ZERO IS YOUR HERO!

Why You Need A "Zero" In Your Retirement Plan

LANCE A. MAYS

*"For my lovely wife Kim.
Thank you for all your support and
patience all these years."*

TABLE OF CONTENTS

FOREWORD AND ACKNOWLEDGEMENTS

This book is as "timely" as its concepts are "timeless". This writing would not be possible without the widespread lack of preparation by most Americans planning for retirement, and the tens of thousands of stockbrokers, investment brokerages, wire houses, financial planners, lawyers, and CPA's plain ignorance of the most ***basic and future needs*** of most retirees now. Yes, really. I'm quite confident I will get emails and push back on that statement alone. If they actually read this book, I'm more than happy to discuss this with any of them at any time.

I'm sure you have heard this, or read this multiple times, about the "unexpected" financial shortfalls in people's retirement planning. We were always told to put money away in 401(k)'s and IRAs. Plan for this, save for that, and sacrifice now because "it will be better when I retire". But what's even worse is the unexpected shock and amazement of the "unknown" – but it's really known and just not talked about in most cases. Yet they are among the deadliest of downfalls... TAXES and HEALTHCARE in retirement. Over 70% of retirees will face a sickness or illness requiring medical care lasting more than 60 days after age 65. If married, there is a 90% chance one of you will need long-term care. Here's the kicker: **100%** of retirees will be required to pay taxes in some form. However, most advisors and brokers do not specialize in that type of planning. Please think about that as you read on.

Disposable income and money in your accounts on a tax-free basis is, in one form or another, imperative. Notice I did not say "tax-favored" like 401(k)'s or IRAs.

I'm speaking of the importance of tax-free money. True industry experts in the field of retirement income planning are far and few between. The information is "out there". But finding it, understanding it, and applying it to your retirement future is another thing, and painfully confusing to most. Have no fear... ZERO is here! It's easier than you think once you read this book.

I say this because most of you reading this have CPA's, bookkeepers, and tax preparers who help you and or file your annual tax returns. The information is out there and available for everyone to file their own taxes. Why don't you? Again, because it's extremely confusing to most people. Just as most advisors have made true and proper retirement planning confusing, remember this paragraph for later reference in our book about what the top wealthiest people do and own for retirement. Just like the IRS advice I just said. It's available to all, just not explained all that well - to all.

Remember, the IRS Code books are accessible to everyone. IRS forms and helpful forums online, even representatives from the IRS to speak with! Yet NOWHERE in the tens of thousands of pages of IRS Code books are the words, **TAX FREE.** Especially in relation to your retirement and retirement income, those two little words, 7 letters, will be among the most powerful you'll ever hear and use after reading this book.

No one I know has a crystal ball to predict the future. But there is one thing that we have all heard time and time again. "Only two things for certain in this world... Death and Taxes".

Taxes will be increasing. There, I said it. I do not care what side of the political aisle you are on. Taxes will go up. They must. It's simple math. Please let this book serve as an eye-opener – a wake-up call to a certain reality in all of our futures.

I'm not saying this as a "prediction". It's 110% certainty, in one form or another.

ARE YOU PREPARED FOR THESE ADDITIONAL EXPENDITURES OUT OF YOUR RETIREMENT DOLLARS?

Our government, especially now, will have no choice but to raise taxes on individuals and businesses. Remember all the Bailouts, Stimulus Packages, Federal Quantitative Easing, and Financial COVID-19 relief aid? You may think, "I don't care about taxes being raised on businesses." But you should. Be very aware that those costs and expenditures put upon businesses will get passed on to you as a consumer. Remember, higher taxes at any level result in less money for you and your financial future. We will cover this in more detail as you progress further into this writing.

This book is for those people planning for retirement, nearing retirement age, or just entering retirement. It's not to cater to the "Sophisticated Financial Advisor or Broker". They've had their chance to get it right for clients, and most of them have not. Enough said about that.

If this book was referred to you by a person in the financial industry, they are trying to educate you on the most important aspects of your retirement and do right by you.

These pages come from my years of both research and real-world experiences with my own clients over a 30-plus-year career. I have given over 700 live speaking engagements in 35 different states. I had a 10-plus-year live, call-in talk radio show called "When Wall Street Meets Mainstreet" with my good friend and co-worker at the time named Adam. I've "seen it all and heard it all" with great Americans from all walks of life, all levels of income, and retirement status.

This book is written for you—the American worker. Either you're in retirement or preparing for retirement, or you should be. Written in easy-to-understand, relatable language. No "sugar coating" or "special terminologies" or industry "speak" and no confusing charts and graphs. I like to say there are two types of people. Those who want to know what time it is... and those who want to know how the watch is made, where it's from, etc., etc. I'm going to tell you what time it is.

It may not be "technical" enough for you to restructure your entire portfolio around, but it will give the starting point and insight required to ask the right questions and begin specific research for your own unique situation. Do not be put off or misled by your current advisors or your own past investment understandings. Just because "something is familiar, doesn't make it right," especially in today's changing times.

Dive in! Read on. Find out why you need a ZERO in your retirement, and **ZERO IS YOUR HERO**.... Or it should be!

DISCLOSURE

The information contained in this book is intended for general informational purposes. Although we consider the content to be reliable and accurate as of the date of publication, it is essential to recognize that individual circumstances may vary significantly.

Accordingly, any information presented should be considered only in conjunction with personalized professional tax and/or financial advice. It is important to evaluate your particular situation, including health and legacy objectives, before acting on any material discussed in this book.

Please be advised that neither the information provided nor any opinions expressed herein constitute an offer to solicit, purchase, or sell any insurance products, securities products, or services referenced in this publication. The information should serve solely as a resource and inspiration to help you work toward enhancing your retirement planning.

This content is not intended to provide tax or legal guidance and should not be relied upon to avoid federal or state tax or potential penalties. Lance Mays, his companies WCI Brokerage, AMC, and employees, and representatives are not authorized to provide tax or legal advice.

We strongly encourage individuals to consult their own tax and legal advisors, as well as financial and/or insurance professionals with similar mindsets, to address their unique needs.

Chapter ONE

THE RECKONING

> *"We must not let our rulers load us with perpetual debt."*
>
> *– Thomas Jefferson letter to Samuel Kercheval, 1816*

In one of my favorite movies, Tombstone, Val Kilmer plays the famous gunslinger Doc Holliday. In one scene, he speaks about a "reckoning" coming. Basically, a settling of "accounts".

In 2025, the U.S. federal government faces a record debt of **$37 plus trillion dollars**, with just annual interest costs now rivaling all defense spending. The "RECKONING" for the United States is inevitable. With America's "Debt Clock" standing at over $37 plus TRILLION DOLLARS, that's roughly $113,000 owed ***per*** US Citizen and growing minute by minute.

Let's put it this way: According to the CBO (Congressional Budget Office), roughly .93 to .94 cents of every dollar the US Government collects in revenue goes to pay just the following: Medicare, Medicaid, Social Security, and Interest on the Debt. What???? Read that again slowly.

What that really means is: we run the entire US Government, All **3** branches, The Park Services, The Secret Service, I.C.E., The National Police Departments, F.D.A., H.U.D., C.D.C., E.P.A., Bureau of Indian Affairs, The Air Force, Coast Guard, Bureau of Land Management, Fish and Wildlife, National Science Foundation, Small Business Administration (S.B.A.), Federal Highway Department, The I.R.S., F.E.M.A., Smithsonian Museums, Federal Student Loans, Housing for the Elderly, Federal Court Systems, The F.B.I., D.E.A., Customs Enforcement, Federal Railroad Administration, National Guard, Federal Food Assistance, The Air Force, The Army, The Navy, The White House, Child Nutrition Programs, Food Safety and Inspection Services, National Transportation Department, NASA, The F.A.A. Just to name a few, ***and***... all the pensions of everyone from these programs, on **.06 to .07 cents of each dollar!** REALLY! Could you manage a business or your home on approximately .06 cents of each dollar? Doubtful.

The government speaks about wanting to reduce Federal spending and not adding more debt. Of course, that's a great starting point. Even as you read this, the Federal Government is collecting record tax receipts and tariffs like never before.

Elon Musk and his DODGE Team found close to $1 trillion in wasteful spending and misappropriated funds, and all of this is barely making a dent in these mandatory obligations. These "unfunded" obligations absorb almost all incoming revenue, leaving huge deficits that must be continually financed by the US Government. How, you ask? By continually borrowing from one sector or another in the form of increased taxes, fees, or "regulations".

As painful as it is, let's take a closer look at these "happy" facts.

Interest alone on the debt now exceeds **$1 trillion annually.** This is larger than the budgets of Medicaid or the Department of Defense. Think of it like this: most people who pay the minimum on their credit cards each month and can't ever seem to catch up or get their balance reduced. Same principle. Same result.

Social Security: The Social Security Trust Fund is projected to be depleted by **2033–2034**. This, of course, has been reported for many years from many sources.

What's the worst thing that could happen? Should Congress fail to address this before the projected OASDI trust fund reaches projected depletion in early 2033 - 2034, current revenues would only cover approximately 77% of scheduled benefits, resulting in an average **23%** reduction to American Seniors. WHAT? (Read that again!)

It is important to note that Social Security will neither go bankrupt nor cease to issue payments because the majority of benefits are financed through ongoing employment tax contributions of existing workers. (Oh, more new taxes on the Americans that are still working? Yup) Now the requirements to receive Social Security are slated to increase, as has the FRA (Full Retirement Age) for maximum benefits for recipients.

In November 2025, the full retirement age (FRA), the age at which individuals are eligible to receive 100% of their Social Security benefits, will increase to 66 years and 10 months for those born in 1959.

In January 2026, several additional changes to Social Security will take effect, impacting everything from credits and taxes to benefit checks and Full Retirement Age (FRA) rules. Knowing about these updates ahead of time can help you understand and be prepared for the years ahead, and adjust your plans to be sure you collect the maximum benefit. These changes don't only impact retirees — they impact current workers. Workers need to keep an eye on accumulating enough Social Security credits to receive future benefits, correct errors in their earnings record, and understand how much of their wages will be subject to the 6.2% Social Security tax. (ssa.gov)

In 2026, the FRA will reach 67 for those born in 1960 or later – a threshold that will mark the culmination of the 42-year-long up shift in raising the retirement age.

This is the final step in a gradual schedule to increase the retirement age from 65 to 67, set in motion by the 1983 amendments to the Social Security Act. The legislation was meant to reflect the new realization of longer life expectancies, reduce financial strain on the program, and shore up the Social Security Trust fund.

Here is, in a nutshell, when you will reach your FRA, by birth year:

- If you were born in 1960 or later, your FRA at this time is age 67.
- If you were born in 1959, your FRA is age 66 and 10 months and is reached in 2025
- If you were born in 1958, your FRA is age 66 and six months, and was reached in 2024

NOTE: People born on January 1 of any year should refer to the previous year.

The main reasons for this are that the number of Americans paying into Social Security has dramatically dropped off. Americans are not having as many children as they used to when the plan was originally enacted. Baby Boomers had close to 32 million fewer children than their parents did! That, with the fact that we're living much longer now than anyone at that time had foreseen.

How Would This Take Place? What Do I Do?

Reductions would occur automatically, as Social Security is legally prohibited from "borrowing" or incurring debt. Legislative postponement remains a possible action until it becomes unavoidable.

I personally feel that "elected" officials would not be reelected if that happened, and they will create "some other" way to fund that - (higher taxes?) to get elected and reelected and point the fingers across the aisle for blame.

***When* you claim your Social Security benefits, it can greatly impact the size of your monthly check.**

As of this writing, if you retire at age 62, the earliest possible Social Security retirement age, your benefit will be lower than if you wait until your Full Retirement Age (FRA). The more months remaining between age 62 and your FRA, the more your monthly payments will be reduced.

Early retirement will reduce your benefits by 5/9 of 1% for each month before normal retirement age, up to 36 months. If the number of months exceeds 36, then the benefit is further reduced by 5/12 of 1% per month.

If you choose to continue working beyond your full retirement age and delay applying for benefits, you can increase future Social Security benefits in two ways:

1. Each extra year you work adds another year of earnings to your Social Security record, and higher lifetime earnings can mean higher benefits when you retire.
2. If you delay taking your benefits, your monthly check will increase for every month you wait, up until age 70. You'll get an extra 2/3 of 1% for each month you delay after your birthday month, adding up to 8% for each full year you wait until age 70. You stop accumulating delayed retirement credits when you turn 70 at this time.

My Insight

Nowadays, medical advancements and healthier lifestyles have pushed the projected life expectancy from 67 at the inception of the Social Security Program to over 84 years old now! Literally meaning that if you retired and started taking Social Security Benefits at 62 or 63 years old, you could almost draw Social Security for nearly a quarter of your life! Remember, Social Security was never intended to be "*Your Retirement Program.*" It was merely a supplement or safeguard for you if you are living too long. Another reason not often talked about is that the number of Americans paying into Social Security went from over 40 people paying in per 1 recipient receiving benefits, to now only 2 or 3 workers paying in to it for one recipient. According to hhs.com, on average, 11,400 people per day will turn 65 in 2025. This phenomenon is referred to as **Peak 65**. This number will have large implications for retirement planning, healthcare, and the economy at large. Again, there are no more increases after age 70. www.ssa.gov can help you determine what is best for you, as well as many qualified advisors who specialize in this area.

- **Medicare:** Because of the overwhelming number of Americans turning 65, Medicare in its present form also faces insolvency within the next decade as health costs continue to rise and fewer people are paying into it as well.
- **Unfortunately, a big increase in Medicare premiums can consume almost half of your Cost-of-Living Adjustment (COLA) Social Security annual increase**. The 2025 Social Security Trustees Report projects a $206.50 monthly premium for next year, up $21.50 or 11.6% from 2025. That would represent the largest Part B increase in dollar terms since 2022, when premiums rose by $21.60 per month.

- Navigating the complexities of Medicare can be daunting. Receive Medicare Parts A and B, or opt for a Medicare Advantage Plan (Part C), or sign up for Medicare Part D or one of many other supplements? A dizzying decision, to say the least.

- The most important thing is **NOT** delaying Medicare enrollment, as it can result in penalties. It is crucial to understand the plans and deadlines to make an informed decision before the enrollment date! It is best to speak with a Medicare expert in this area. (**Note**, please do not think that Medicare will help you with any Long-Term Care needs. Medicare ***does not*** cover long-term care, particularly custodial care or nursing home stays. It can cover some short-term skilled nursing care in a Skilled Nursing Facility (SNF) for a limited time following a hospital stay, and some home health care services. For long-term custodial care, which helps with daily activities, you'll likely need to pay out-of-pocket, seek assistance from a long-term care insurance policy, or explore programs like Medicaid (which has strict income and asset requirements) or the Department of Veterans Affairs if you are a Veteran. You may need to investigate LTC supplemental insurances or one of the other insurance-related products discussed in later chapters.

- Remember, at the beginning, I stated, "unknown or unacknowledged or unexpected expenses when you retire?" ***Ta Daa***, these can be as much or more than taxes. Depending upon where you live, your required medical needs care, stay at home care, or in a facility, your costs are as much as $8,000 to $20,000 per month! The average Alzheimer's patient is 8 years in specialized care. Is your retirement portfolio able to handle that? If not, please read on.

These programs are governmental obligations. These programs are "non-negotiable" promises to voters and political suicide to politicians who want to change these programs but do not want to fund changes to these programs. Simple ***math*** suggests that future generations are most likely to face much higher tax rates, reduced benefits, or both if these programs are not attended to very soon.

WHERE'S THE MONEY TO FIX THIS GOING TO COME FROM?

This matters for Retirees and those planning on retiring soon. Now more than ever, it's the right time to strategically plan your retirement. You need to plan your future tax situation as well as your income situation so you can keep more of your hard-earned money. We will cover this more in-depth in future chapters, but we need to put this out there for you to think about now as we move forward.

- Remember, the government controls the tax rate applied to every dollar in your tax-deferred accounts and ultimately your retirement income (traditional IRAs, 401(k)s).
- Today's rates (10–37%) are historically low, preserved by the ***One Big Beautiful Bill*** (**OBBB**), but those reductions face phasing out in 2029–2030 for many of the provisions. So literally now it's like **"*taxes are on sale*"** now!
- If Congress is forced to raise revenue, retirement accounts could become the easiest targets because trillions and trillions of dollars are in deferred retirement accounts. They represent "untaxed income" waiting to be tapped. In the government's mind, it's not your money (well, not all of it, that's for sure).

THE OBBB WINDOW OF OPPORTUNITY

The ***One Big Beautiful Bill*** was passed in 2025. It has extended the Trump-era brackets and deductions, giving taxpayers breathing room for a while. But there is most likely a big storm brewing. We could be in the proverbial "calm before the storm". What does that mean to you?

- Enhanced **standard deductions** ($15,750 single / $31,500 joint, plus $6,000 senior bump) expire after 2028.
- Expanded **SALT caps** (State and local Taxes) and **charitable deductions** will also roll back by 2030.
- After the mid-term elections in 2026, many experts forecast that the 2028 Presidential elections will focus on fixing and funding Medicare and Social Security. Shouldn't it?
- If rates rise, conversions that looked expensive today will seem like bargains tomorrow. Debt pressures + mandatory entitlement costs + political resistance to benefit cuts = rising likelihood of higher taxes. (Psst... Taxes are on sale now!)
- Today's historically favorable rates, boosted by OBBB reforms, are not permanent.
- Retirees must assume that future withdrawals from tax-deferred accounts will be taxed at higher rates than today. (Psst... Taxes are on sale now!)

If you act under the assumption that taxes **will** rise:

- Every dollar shifted into tax-free vehicles now is a hedge against future government policy.
- Building a "**ZERO** - 0% tax bracket retirement" is less about speculation and more about arithmetic: the government cannot meet obligations without new revenue. (Psst... Taxes are on sale now!)
- The true cost of inaction may be far greater than the temporary pain of Roth conversions or funding a LIRP today if you qualify. More on that in future chapters.
- (Psst... Taxes are on sale now!)

The storm is closer, bigger, and costlier than previously thought. The 2025 tax code has given us a rare window of calm—but just like in oceans and lakes around the world, calm waters don't last forever. Wise retirees will use this period to position themselves in the 0% tax bracket before the winds of change pick up again.

What Are The Best Options For Your Money?

It's not only important, but irresponsible, not to create a financial and retirement plan that looks at and addresses as many of the possibilities in the future as you can. In daily living and retirement planning, every dollar you've saved will ultimately fall into one of three areas or "buckets": taxable, tax-deferred, or tax-free. How you allocate between them determines not just your lifetime tax bill, but also how secure your retirement will feel in a world of rising fiscal pressures and uncertain taxes in the future.

Potential Savings/Investment Vehicles To Consider

Stock Market and Insurance-based Retirement, Saving, and Investment Products

- Stocks
- Bonds
- Mutual Funds
- Market-Based Annuity
- Variable Annuity
- Indexed Annuity

These financial products and investment options are connected to the performance of the stock and bond markets in different ways:

- Stocks: Shares of ownership in companies, offering growth potential and risk based on market fluctuations.
- Bonds: Debt securities issued by corporations or governments, generally providing regular interest payments with lower risk than stocks, but also subject to market changes.
- Mutual Funds: Investment vehicles that pool money from multiple investors to buy a diversified portfolio of stocks, bonds, or other assets. Returns and risks depend on the fund's holdings.
- Market-Based Annuity, Variable Annuity, Indexed Annuity: Insurance-based products that link growth potential to market index performances, with varying degrees of risk and complexity. These are designed for retirement

planning and may offer income guarantees, lifetime income, and may have limited upside, but no downside risk.

When choosing among these options, it's important to consider your goals, risk tolerance, time horizon, and whether you prefer direct investments (like stocks and mutual funds) or insurance-based solutions (like annuities) that provide additional features such as income guarantees or downside protection.

Chapter TWO

TODAY MONEY
THE TAXABLE BUCKET

> *"Better to have a permanent income than be fascinating!"*
>
> *— Oscar Wilde*

This is the most common "bucket" people know and yet do not understand fully. This is money that has already been taxed. Sometimes referred to as after-tax money. So, any gains, interest earned, dividends, and capital gains would be taxable to you going forward. This includes checking and savings accounts, CDs, money market accounts, Brokerage Accounts, alternative investments, and Crypto accounts; all of these would be considered a taxable account. (Assuming they were not within a retirement account)

You can easily identify taxable investments by the annual tax documents sent to you each year-end by financial institutions. At the end of each year, you will receive a Form 1099, which serves as a summary of the taxable income generated from these accounts. The IRS uses this information to assess what portion of your investment growth is subject to tax.

For example, if you place $100,000 in a CD and it grows by 4% annually, the account will show a balance of $104,000 after one year. However, the entire $4,000 growth is considered taxable income. This amount is added to your overall income, and you are taxed according to the highest marginal tax rate. If the combined federal and state tax rate is 30% (composed of 24% federal and say a 6% state tax), the tax owed would total $1,200.

After accounting for taxes, the actual growth realized from the investment is only $2,800, reducing the effective rate of return to less than 4%. This shows you a key disadvantage of taxable accounts: the annual taxation of these accounts reduces the net gains, impacting the overall growth of your investments and increasing your future tax bills. Another "silent killer" to add to this mix is inflation. Add 3% inflation to the 30% in State and Federal taxes, and you're looking at real losses.

While useful for liquidity and emergencies, this bucket is highly inefficient for long-term growth. This money is your **"Today"** money. Used for day-to-day, week-to-week, and month-to-month living expenses. Generally speaking, this money is set aside for a maximum of up to 12 months' worth of living expenses. Any longer and your growth will most likely be eaten up by taxes. This growth does create a future tax consequence from money that was already taxed before, and that growth (gain) is taxed and treated as ordinary income, which could impact the taxation of your Social Security Benefits. Confusing, isn't it?

Quick summary: these are the most common accounts for taxation on taxable short-term money.

- **Interest** is taxed annually at ordinary income rates (10–37%).
- **Dividends** may be taxed at 0%, 15%, or 20%, depending on income.

- **Capital gains** are taxed when realized, with long-term gains often at 15–20%.
- **It could affect the taxation of your Social Security checks.**

Money in these accounts long-term is considered as "tax ticking time bombs".

Chapter THREE

SOMEDAY MONEY

THE TAX-DEFERRED BUCKET

"I am more concerned about the return of my money – than the return on my money."

– Will Rogers

Most of us have been told our entire working life, defer... defer... defer, because "when" you retire, you'll be in a lower tax bracket. Sound familiar? Perhaps your own "advisor" spoke like this to you. Unless you're a multi-millionaire and don't mind giving money away to Uncle Sam, get a new advisor, pronto! Find one that truly understands retirement planning, deferred taxes, "unforeseen medical expenses," and tax efficiency (tax-free) as a retiree. The mantra defer, defer, defer statement may have been true 20 - 30 years ago, but if you believe that taxes will increase in the future (inevitable that they will), you will inherently pay higher taxes than you would when you were working or even now. Which, of course, goes against the mantra of the "defer taxes" statement.

At its simplest form, this money is money that has yet to be taxed. Sometimes this is referred to as before-tax money, or qualified money. This is money you have planned to use **"Someday"**. It has been growing on a "pre-tax" basis. This is the kind of account the government **LOVES** you to have! The "upside" is that contributions are tax-deductible in the year you contribute. So, if you earn $100,000 this year and put $10,000 in the IRA, your new taxable income is only $90,000. So, your money is making money, which hopefully creates more money, and the government hopes you do as well, and more future taxes than when you started this whole deferred account.

The "downside" is that if you withdraw any money from this account, it would be considered as "income" and all of it, including the growth, would be taxable at the *ordinary income tax level* for the year in which you withdraw the money.

Another "downside" is that if your qualified/pretax account loses value, you cannot take a deduction on your taxes, as you "technically" don't own it and do not have the full rights to the money yet, because it hasn't been taxed yet. So, if you are taking distributions monthly or annually of 10%, and the market goes down 15%, you now have 25% less money in your account and no recourse or deduction on taxes. We will address a strategy to safeguard against this in the upcoming chapters.

Most seniors heading into retirement years had a very frustrating moment when they realized the "story" they were told most of their adult working life about "being in a lower tax bracket" when they retire, had been a lie. Not malicious, or on purpose, but it's still not true in over 80% of seniors' lives.

The reality is that when you retire, most likely you will lose the main reasons you were able to reduce your taxes when you were working. Nowhere in the entire IRS Tax Code do the words "Tax Breaks" or "Write-offs" occur. Exclusions, deductions, and credits are all they speak about. Like it or not, as a retiree, you're about to lose the biggest deductions most people have ever had.

This "Ahh–Haa" moment is both good and bad. It shows you that now could be a great opportunity to move money around before it is too late or becomes too expensive with higher taxes looming in the future. (Psst.... Taxes are on sale now!)

You can bet your bottom dollar the government is out there looking for all avenues of more revenue and eyeing the $47 plus TRILLION dollars in deferred retirement plans that are invested in American workers' retirement plans. With the changes that have already been made and the 2019 SECURE ACT and SECURE ACT 2.0 in 2022, it certainly looks like retirement accounts will figure into the mix sooner rather than later.

Consequently, early preparation is essential. Many individuals assume rising taxes will not affect them, but historical data demonstrate otherwise. Believe it or not, federal income tax rates have previously surpassed 90%! From 1936 to 1981, the top tax rates remained above 70%. Higher rates directly reduce retirement savings and quality of life. Will it happen to that extent? I'm doubtful. Could it happen to a lesser extent? Based on simple mathematics, it must.

Year	Top Marginal Tax Rate (%)
1920	73
1930	25
1940	81
1944–1945	94
1950	91
1960	91
1970	71.75
1980	70
1986	50
1988	28
1990	28
1993	39.6
2003	35
2013	39.6
2018	37
2024 - 2025 same	37

This chart summarizes the highest U.S. federal income tax rates over the past century, showing dramatic increases during the mid-20th century, followed by significant reductions from the 1980s onward. Recent decades have seen relative stability in the top marginal rate, hovering between 35% and 39.6%. But for how much longer?

Below, I have listed the **4** main deductions most adults who itemize their deductions on their taxes lose when they retire. See how this may apply to you.

Mortgage Interest: When you itemize deductions, you look for where you can legally deduct expenses from your taxes. The largest deduction for most seniors has been that they can deduct up to $750,000 of mortgage interest each year. However, most of the seniors/retirees I have worked with have already paid off their homes, so they lose this personal deduction. So, the largest source of a deduction is nonexistent for many retired Americans.

Children as Tax Credits: Children can provide significant tax savings by qualifying for a tax credit. Unlike deductions, which reduce taxable income, a credit directly reduces the amount of tax owed. For example, in July 2025, the tax credit has been raised to $2,200 per eligible child. However, if children are living with you during retirement, they may no longer meet the criteria to be counted as dependents. (Unless you're just helping them out for a while, you'd hope they aren't living with you! Am I right?)

Retirement Plan Contributions: Individuals typically do not contribute to their 401(k) or IRA during retirement. These accounts are intended for withdrawals after retirement, rather than ongoing contributions for tax deductions. That also could be creating a larger tax bill for you or your heirs.

Charity: While charitable intentions are great and often persist throughout retirement. Financial resources may become more limited, especially for those on a fixed income. Consequently, individuals more frequently contribute their time rather than their money for donations. For example, instead of providing financial support to a church or special cause you're passionate about, retirees may personally volunteer at the organization instead of writing a check. Although this form of contribution is admirable and valuable, it is not recognized as a "deductible" activity by the IRS.

REVIEW: These are the most common types of tax-deferred-qualified accounts that most people recognize:

- Traditional IRAs
- 401(k)s, 403(b)s, TSPs
- SEP and SIMPLE IRAs
- ROTH IRAs

Now these accounts have grown massively thanks to decades of employee contributions, employer contributions, and market gains. The catch? They represent future **untaxed income** to you, and your favorite uncle, Uncle Sam (the government), is patiently waiting to collect. The longer you defer, the more the tax grows on the accounts, and the government loves that.

More than likely, you were planning on spending some of your tax-deferred retirement accounts, but at a withdrawal rate and a tax rate ***you*** thought you'd be in control of. Maybe a systematic monthly or quarterly check. Or perhaps not even touch it at all and pass it on to your heirs. Not so fast. The government has other ideas and wants/needs their "fair share" in their opinion.

As a matter of fact, many seniors I've worked with do not need the money in their IRAs when they retire. Simply put, they're downright angry in some cases. The potential "problem" is that once you become 73 years old, whether you want to or not, you lose control of how much you want to take out, and at the tax rate you perhaps wanted.

You probably know this as "RMDs – Required Minimum Distributions". You are required to withdraw money from your tax-deferred accounts at a percentage the IRS has dictated. This figure is based upon your tax-deferred account balance on December 31st of the preceding year. This percentage goes up every year, so you must "spend through" your IRA / pretax dollars account over your golden senior years. No matter the tax consequences, or even if you need it or not.

Below is the current IRS Uniform Lifetime Table used to determine Required Minimum Distributions (RMDs) for most account owners. The distribution period factor corresponds to your age as of December 31 of the year of distribution, applied to your prior year-end account balance.

By the way, if you are married and your spouse has their own IRA, the same applies to them! So, you could theoretically double these figures.

Age	Distribution Period Factor	RMD Calculation Example on ($100,000 Balance)
73	26.5	$100,000 : 26.5 = $3,774
74	25.5	$100,000 : 25.5 = $3,922
75	24.6	$100,000 : 24.6 = $4,065
76	23.7	$100,000 : 23.7 = $4,219
77	22.9	$100,000 : 22.9 = $4,367
78	22.0	$100,000 : 22.0 = $4,545
79	21.1	$100,000 : 21.1 = $4,739
80	20.2	$100,000 : 20.2 = $4,950
85	16.0	$100,000 : 16.0 = $6,250
90	11.4	$100,000 : 11.4 = $8,772
95	8.6	$100,000 : 8.6 = $11,628

To calculate your annual RMD, divide the prior year-end balance of your IRA or 401(k) by the distribution period factor shown for your age. The complete table is published by the IRS and covers all ages up to 120.

If you withdraw the wrong amount, or just don't do it, you face stiff penalties or fines of 50% of what you were supposed to take out, plus pay taxes on top of that, and still need to take the money out! In some cases, this "unwanted" income could cause a taxation of up to 85% of your Social Security and potentially push you into a higher tax bracket.

So, your hand really gets forced here. You must take money you perhaps don't want or need and pay whatever the income tax rates are. We have several solutions to this potential problem in future chapters, such as keeping only enough in this bucket so that, when RMDs begin, they don't push you into higher tax brackets or trigger penalties, or better yet, be proactive in younger years to reposition money into tax-free accounts. (Psst.... Taxes are on sale now!) Remember, "It's hard to get hit by a train, the tax train... if you're not on the tracks!"

Summary

- Required Minimum Distributions **(RMDs)** begin at age 73, whether you want to or not.
- Withdrawals/distributions are taxed as ordinary income—at whatever brackets Congress sets in the future. If you don't take the correct amount, you are penalized.
- Large IRA, pretax account balances can trigger "tax chain reactions": higher RMDs → higher taxable Social Security → possible Medicare IRMAA surcharges. IRMAA is an additional charge that some higher-income Medicare beneficiaries pay for their Medicare Part B.

EXAMPLE CASE

Imagine a couple with $1.5 million in their 401(k)s. By age 75, their RMD could exceed **$75,000 annually**—even if they don't need the income. This additional income might:

- Push them into the 24% bracket or higher
- Cause up to 85% of Social Security benefits to become taxable
- Trigger **Medicare Part B and D surcharges** (IRMAA), adding thousands in annual premiums
- Literally, you can "have *more* with less money" when it's tax-free. A quick example I use to share with clients is, "I would rather have $700,000 in a tax-free account than $1,000,000 in an IRA account". Especially if you live in a state that has state income tax! Wouldn't you?

Currently, tax rates are historically low, presenting an opportune moment to establish tax-free income streams for retirement and future generations. Various legal provisions exist within the tax code to help you get tax-free retirement income, yet they remain way underutilized. Roth IRAs and life insurance products, for instance, offer avenues for increasing and protecting family wealth while reducing future tax liability.

Moving assets from forever-taxed accounts to never-taxed accounts is critical. Building tax-free savings now ensures greater protection for retirement wealth and stability. Tax-free accounts are the first "**ZERO**" we allude to in the book title, and the most important ZERO in my opinion, that ***you*** can control and need in your life!

It is prudent to recognize that taxes are most likely to rise, and tax-deferred accounts may become increasingly vulnerable to higher tax rates.

By implementing the recommendations presented in this book, you can safeguard your retirement savings from excessive taxation. Tax-free planning offers distinct advantages, helping individuals retain more of their earnings and a predictable retirement budget. (Pssst... taxes are on sale now!)

If you are uncertain whether you have a strategy to minimize current and future income taxes, it is unlikely that you do not possess one now. Without proactive measures, retirees will default to government-prescribed plans, which will not serve their retirement's best interests. Taxes.

Individuals must develop and implement their own strategies promptly. Well before any increases occur. “Hindsight” is no sight going forward - except regret!

Update Note - September 30, 2025

There have been very significant and recent changes to the 401(k) and ROTH and ROTH “catch-up rule”, originally set to take effect in 2024, was postponed to January 1, 2026, according to IRS Notice 2023-62 (initial guidance on the Roth and 401(k) catch-up rule). This delay has provided much-needed relief to employers to change the plans for workers to contribute to their retirement accounts and to “make up” financial ground for their retirement.

This mostly affects high earners who make more than $145,000 per year. Please consult your plan administrators and or CPA’s as to the amounts you can contribute based upon your income and deduct from your gross income.

The rule must be in place by January 1, 2026, but the proposed regulations issued on January 10, 2025, will apply to tax years starting six months after the final regulations are published. For example, if the final regulations are published on July 20, 2026, then plans must comply with them beginning January 1, 2028. There may be further delays for certain collectively bargained plans. From January 1, 2026, until that regulatory applicability date, retirement plan administrators should follow a reasonable, good-faith interpretation of SECURE 2.0 and IRS Notice 2023-62.

As I've stated, changes are happening in the retirement income world designed to increase revenue for the government. This is only the beginning. Please stay informed and get into a TAX-FREE, NEVER TAXED ACCOUNT!

Chapter FOUR

THE TAX-FREE BUCKET

> *I love tax-free, and you will too. Tax-free is always better! Pay less and keep more!*

This is the first **ZERO** I wrote about earlier. This is where the real magic for a retirement account and your financial future happens! Simply put, this is money that has already been taxed and is now growing tax-free, and the distributions are also tax-free. We will refer to this "Bucket" as the Tax-Free Bucket.

Question For You To Think About

I was originally born and raised in Iowa. I know a thing or two about farming and crops. I grew up working hard on various farms in our area.

If you were a farmer, would you rather be taxed on the "seed" of what you are going to plant, or the bounty of the entire field at the end of the harvest? It is a pretty simple question, but it explains this concept quite well.

When you first began your saving and investing journey, accounts such as a 401(k), 403(b), various versions of IRAs, or a 457 were the most common options, and more than likely, there may not have been a ROTH (or tax-free) option available then.

Be cautious with this one; many investments are marketed as tax-free, but to truly earn that label, an investment must meet two key criteria.

First, the investment must be entirely free from federal, state, and capital gains taxes. Municipal bonds, for example, are often labeled tax-free, but this isn't always the case. The interest may be federally tax-free, but not always state tax-free, unless you invest in bonds issued by your own state. Additionally, profits from selling municipal bond mutual funds can incur capital gains tax, meaning these bonds don't always provide true tax-free benefits.

Second, distributions from the investment should not count as "provisional income". This means they won't be factored into calculations that could cause your Social Security benefits to be taxed. Even though interest from municipal bonds is often touted as tax-free, it still counts as provisional income and may influence the taxation of your Social Security. Yes, there are limits on how much you can earn without affecting the taxation of your Social Security. If you earn too much from investment income, in the wrong type of account, up to 85% of your Social Security is taxed at ordinary income levels.

This is called Provisional Income.

Filing Status	Provisional Income Range	Percentage of Social Security Taxable
Single	Less than $25,000	0%
Single	$25,000 to $34,000	Up to 50%
Single	More than $34,000	Up to 85%
Married Filing Jointly	Less than $32,000	0%
Married Filing Jointly	$32,000 to $44,000	Up to 50%
Married Filing Jointly	More than $44,000	Up to 85%

Provisional income includes your adjusted gross income, non-taxable interest, and half of your Social Security benefits. If your income exceeds these thresholds, a larger portion of your Social Security benefits will be subject to ordinary income tax rates. “WHAT? Are you kidding me?”

No, no, I’m not. This gets back to making sure you position yourself the right way, with the right products and accounts moving forward.

The Roth IRA

The ROTH Individual Retirement Account (ROTH IRA) stands out as a fan favorite tax-free investment. It passes both tests—so long as you have owned it at least 5 years and you’re at least 59½. All withdrawals are free from federal, state, and capital gains taxes, and they do not count as provisional income. This means ROTH IRA distributions won’t cause your Social Security to be taxed.

ROTH IRA contributions are made with after-tax dollars, so you will not get a tax deduction upfront. However, your investments grow tax-free, and qualified withdrawals remain tax-free, and no RMDs are required. Yes, you can contribute to both a ROTH IRA and a regular 401(k) / IRA, subject to contribution guidelines. (A smart play is to have both. Vest in your employers' contributions and then, as you are old enough and financially able, begin converting some of your 401(k) / IRA to a ROTH, especially when the government begins to speak about tax increases.)

There are, however, some constraints: The main constraint is that the IRS imposes annual contribution limits. As of 2025, if you're under 50, you can contribute up to $7,000 per year to a ROTH, and those 50 and older can add a catch-up contribution for a total of $8,000. ***The lower Roth IRA limits reflect its value as a tax-free vehicle.***

There is another ROTH vehicle available in the marketplace, but honestly, very few employers offer this to their employees. It's called a ROTH 401(k). Below are the comparisons of both ROTH's.

Roth Ira Vs. Roth 401(K) Contribution Limits And Rules For 2025

- Account Type: Roth IRA / Roth 401(k)
- Maximum Annual Contribution (Under 50): $7,000 (IRA) / $23,000 (401(k)
- Catch-Up Contribution (Age 50+): +$1,000 (IRA) / +$7,500 (401(k)
- Total Allowed (Age 50+): $8,000 (IRA) / $30,500 (401(k)

- Income Limits (Married Filing Jointly): $230,000 (IRA phase-out) / No income limit (401(k)
- Income Limits (Single): $153,000 (IRA phase-out) / No income limit (401(k)
- Tax Deduction Upfront: No deductions for either (IRA & 401(k)
- Qualified Withdrawals: Tax-free for both, if account held 5+ years and age 59½+
- Required Minimum Distributions (RMDs): None (IRA) / Required (401(k), unless still working)
- Employer Contributions: Not allowed (IRA) / Allowed (401(k); employer match goes into traditional 401(k), and you will be taxed on the employer's match.)
- Contribution Source: After-tax dollars for both (IRA & 401(k)
- Withdrawal Rules: Contributions may be withdrawn penalty-free at any time for IRA; earnings are subject to restrictions for both. Predominantly, your age and how long you've owned it.
- Retirees and those without earned income are ineligible to contribute.

HIGHLIGHTS

- ROTH IRA: Lower contribution limits, subject to income caps, no RMDs, no employer contributions.
- ROTH 401(k): Higher contribution limits, no income caps, RMDs apply, employer contributions permitted (but go into traditional 401(k) but you are taxed on their contribution.

- Bottom line is ROTH 401(k)s are not nearly as popular as a traditional ROTH IRA or 401(k). Why... because most people like to delay paying the tax now. (Remember the mantra defer... defer... defer?) Not the best move in my opinion if you truly believe taxes will go up in the future. Obviously, "***if***" taxes stay the same, no harm no foul. But "***if***" taxes increase even 2% more in the future, you will have regret.

Note: IRS guidelines may change; verify the latest limits and regulations at the official IRS website or with your tax advisor. Further, I would strongly advise speaking to your tax professional about proper reporting of a ROTH 401(k), especially when it comes to withdrawals and RMD, or no RMD, and whether it affects your Social Security payments and taxes, as we covered earlier under Provisional Income. It currently says "*both*" in the IRS Guidelines; it is then suggested you "roll it" to a regular ROTH IRA to avoid that.

ROTH IRA INCOME LIMITS

Not everyone can contribute to and begin a ROTH. High earners are restricted. Married couples earning over $189,000 (singles over $120,000) will see their ability to contribute phase out. Additionally, to contribute, you must have earned income, so retirees or those without a paycheck are ineligible.

LIQUIDITY CONSTRAINTS

You can access your Roth IRA contributions anytime, but to withdraw investment growth tax-free, you must have held the account for at least five years and be at least 59½. Early withdrawals of earnings may result in taxes and penalties, and withdrawn funds cannot be redeposited for future growth.

Despite these restrictions, the value of the Roth IRA lies in these very limits. Congress and the IRS only allow so much access to such a beneficial account. "If it's too good to be true... (you know the rest) - there's a catch."

With these definitions in mind, let's look at all investments that qualify as truly tax-free.

- ROTH IRAs & ROTH 401(k)s
- Life Insurance Retirement Plans (LIRPs), when structured correctly
- Municipal bonds (though not always fully tax-free at the state level)

These accounts allow for **tax-free growth, tax-free distributions, and tax-free transfer to heirs**. Importantly, (except Municipal Bonds) **don't count toward provisional income**, meaning they don't make Social Security taxable or trigger Medicare penalties.

SEP IRAs (Self-Employed IRAs) permit up to the lesser of $66,000 or 25% of total compensation. Distributions will also count towards Provisional Income and potentially cause your Social Security Benefits to be taxed.

There you go. I thought you should know and be aware, but they do not accomplish what we are trying to do here. Which is getting to the **ZERO** tax rate on Social Security income and retirement income. These accounts are not without merit and need, as I will go into in future chapters.

Current Advantage

Because tax rates are **historically low through 2028 under OBBB**, this is the window to move assets from **tax-deferred →**

tax-free via ROTH conversions or LIRP funding is unprecedented.

- Converting $100,000 now might cost you $22,000 in taxes (if in the 22% bracket).
- If tax rates rise in the future, that same conversion could cost **$32,000 or more!**
- It may make sense to pay the tax once now, at historically low rates, then never pay tax again. Perhaps even do systematic withdrawals now and pay tax as you go.

Proposed Ideal Strategy - The Three Buckets Allocations

Bucket	Example Accounts	Tax Treatment	Ideal Allocation
Taxable	Checking, savings, CDs, brokerage	Taxed annually (interest, dividends, gains)	5–10% (liquidity only)
Tax-Deferred	Traditional IRA, 401(k), TSP	Taxed later at ordinary income + RMDs	"Just enough" to avoid higher bracket creep
Tax-Free	Roth IRA, Roth 401(k), LIRP	Never taxed again, no impact on Social Security/Medicare	The majority of your money

The key is **balance**. The taxable bucket covers short-term needs. The tax-deferred bucket covers current tax deductions but must be pruned before RMDs hit. Every dollar unnecessarily left here is a dollar you've volunteered for the IRS to tax. The tax-free bucket is where your true long-term security and "peace of mind" lie. Freedom from unknown tax liabilities. Shift excess funds into tax-free accounts where compounding can work its magic through the years, compounding unimpeded, and most importantly, tax-free.

Every dollar you move to the tax-free bucket is an act of future proofing: no matter what Congress does. No matter how high tax rates climb, those dollars remain protected and growing – as Never Taxed!

Chapter FIVE

THE LIRP!

RULE #1 - *Never lose money*

RULE #2 - *See Rule #1*

- *Warren Buffett*

If I could have this chapter be in flashing neon lights, glowing, vibrating, and highlighted, I would. Quite literally, for most Americans, this particular product would solve over 80% plus of all their retirement concerns. Achieving a tax-free retirement represents a significant challenge for many individuals. While conventional instruments such as ROTH IRAs and other tax-advantaged accounts offer notable benefits, they are often subject to restrictions regarding contributions and income eligibility. When you have these limitations, they hamper the pursuit of a ZERO - 0% tax bracket during retirement.

Because of that, alternative solutions must be considered. The Life Insurance Retirement Plan (LIRP) stands out as a particularly effective yet underutilized vehicle for building wealth, preserving wealth, and passing on wealth within a tax-advantaged and tax-free framework.

This chapter offers a comprehensive analysis of the distinctive features and advantages of LIRPs, providing insight into their growing appeal among discerning investors and high-net-worth individuals. Actually, anyone can use it! Really! This is the ultimate in leveraging your dollars for benefits from day one.

What do I mean? Once your plan goes into effect, the very next day, if you "get hit by a car" or have a heart attack and pass away, no matter how much you put into beginning the plan, your family receives the Death Benefit, tax-free, probate-free, in cash within 30 days. That's unbeatable leverage. That's the beauty of Life Insurance in its most basic form. But wait, there's more. A lot more.

According to the Federal Reserve survey data, 24% of assets accumulated tax-free in whole-life and universal-life policies (permanent life plans) are held by the wealthiest 18% of U.S. families as of 2023. Those with more than $5 million in net worth really see the value for estate planning and tax-free asset transfer (think of The Rockefeller method). More broadly, 55% of the assets in such policies were held by the top 25% wealthiest families.

Further, the top 30% of all Fortune 500 CEO's and executives, almost all members of Congress, and the House all utilize this "secret" wealth accumulation plan. I'd bet many of you have never heard of it. Am I right? Remember, earlier I said, "Why don't you do your own taxes?" The information is out there ... but most of you rely on a true professional to do your taxes. I do too, and that's why you're reading my book. To learn how and take advantage of the largest "loophole" in the IRS Code.

This information has been around for a very long time, over 100 years. However, there's a very good chance your advisors are either unfamiliar, uninformed, or have a prejudice against it. Mostly because it reduces their commissions and assets under management (AUM).

Let me break it down for you. Then, if you decide that the wealthiest families in the world, the world's most powerful executives, members of government, high-level employees of the largest corporations in the world, all who use this product, are wrong, so be it. But I'm betting most likely you'll decide that perhaps you need to use it also!

What Is A LIRP?

A Life Insurance Retirement Plan (LIRP) refers to a type of life insurance policy structured to optimize the legal accumulation of cash value within the policy's growth account. (Not a Term Policy) That's the simplest way I can say it.

In contrast to traditional life insurance, which emphasizes providing the maximum death benefit at minimal cost, the LIRP is designed to *minimize* the death benefit to the minimum allowed value in relation to how much you wish to deposit, under IRS guidelines. Notice I said "deposit". This is not an "investment". Investment implies potential loss or risk. This program does not work if you do not follow the guidelines of the plan.

If I could give you a savings vehicle that will accept all the money you want to deposit, have it accumulating tax-free, give you an income for life if you choose completely tax-free, a tax-free death benefit, and tax-free long-term care type coverage ... how much would you put in it? The least? Or the most? Duuuh!

The real focus is on maximizing premium contributions as allowed by IRS regulations. Consequently, this policy primarily serves as a vehicle for tax-advantaged accumulation and tax-free distribution, with life insurance coverage as a supplementary benefit that keeps it legal and within the IRS guidelines.

Key Features Of A LIRP

- Tax-Free Accumulation
- Tax-Free Distributions
- Tax-Free Death Benefit
- Absence of Contribution Limits
- No Income Restrictions
- Minimal Legislative Risk
- Grandfathering Protection for Established Policies
- Provisional Income Exclusion
- Asset Protection and guaranteed growth
- Flexible Access to Cash Value
- Additional Living Benefits -LTC (this is a spectacular feature we will cover in-depth)

What Type Of Insurance Is This?

There are many types of Life Insurance. Whole Life, Term Life, Universal Life, Variable Life, and Indexed Universal Life (IUL) are all types of life insurance that can and do serve a purpose. The one I will be referring to and using in the LIRP is the IUL. It is most recommended by Life Insurance Companies and strongly suggested for the LIRP Program. Mostly because it is the most stable platform that offers account guarantees, cash value, overall growth, can offer flexible premiums, adjustable death benefits, and low fees, and tax-free withdrawals and death benefits. It also lends itself to the ZERO concept, with ZERO losses ever recorded in your cash accumulation account.

I'm often asked, "Ok, how does it credit growth on my money in my account?"

You allocate funds to an accumulation account whose performance is tied to the performance or increases in a stock market index, such as the S&P 500. Crediting returns are based on those returns of the index, such as the S&P 500, ***without*** directly investing in the market. Account holders can benefit from index growth up to a specified cap, generally ranging from 10% to 14%.

Conversely, in periods where the index declines, the account is credited with zero, ensuring that its value does not decrease. Historically back-tested returns have averaged between 7% and 9% crediting, making this strategy a conservative yet effective approach to accumulating tax-advantaged retirement savings.

The method may seem a little more complicated than it needs to be, so let me simplify it. Your account will most likely have one or more of the following.

- Participation Rate: That determines how much of the index gain is credited to your account. For example, a 60% participation rate would credit 60% of the index's gain. There is usually also a Cap Rate of how much of the gain you can receive.
- Cap Rate: Sets the maximum interest you can earn in a given period, most often around 10-14% annually.
- These Participation Rates and Cap Rates are a good thing. Really. You are giving up a little of the upside growth, but you never suffer downside or negative returns, even if the market has been negative for years! The worst you would receive would be zero that year. No loss of principal or previous gains. (ZERO is your Hero again!)

- Floor Rate: Guarantees that your account will not lose value, perhaps even make a little, based on the overall contract guarantees. So, even if the index is negative for a while, no worry of principal or previous earnings lost. The floor credited rate is usually 1% to 3% of the contract. Maybe not a lot, but much better than loss of principal and gains!

Crediting is typically calculated using one of several methods:

- Annual Point-to-Point: Compares the index value at the start and end of the year.
- Monthly Sum or Average: The sums or averages of each month's index performance over the year.
- High Water Mark: Credits interest based on the highest value of the index during the period compared to the start.

These methods offer great upside potential with complete downside protection.

TAX-FREE DISTRIBUTIONS

One aspect of a LIRP is the possibility to take income (distributions) that are not subject to state or federal income tax, including before retirement age if necessary. If structured appropriately, withdrawals from the cash value can be accessed via policy loans, which the IRS ***does not*** treat as taxable income. This differs from distributions from traditional retirement accounts, which are taxed as ordinary income. In addition, these distributions are ***not*** included in provisional income for Social Security purposes and therefore do not affect the taxation of Social Security benefits. So, this could have a very positive impact on overall retirement income. (Psst ... think ZERO is your Hero again!)

No Contribution Limits

Traditional retirement vehicles such as ROTH IRAs are subject to annual contribution limits, as we covered earlier. For example, as of 2025, Roth IRA contributions were limited to $7,000 per year for individuals under 50, and $8,000 for those 50 and older. These limits may restrict the ability to move larger sums into tax-advantaged accounts. Remember, the restrictions on ROTHs are because it's such a great vehicle and the government misses out on future growth... for now.

However, LIRPs follow different regulatory guidelines. While the IRS requires that premium contributions align with the policy's death benefit to prevent misuse of tax advantages, there is no fixed annual maximum on contributions. This allows more flexibility when allocating assets into a tax-advantaged environment. ROTHs and the LIRP are such great programs that the government limits how much cash is put in a ROTH, but the only restriction on the LIRP is based on how much life insurance you have associated with it.

No Income Limits

ROTH IRAs also have income eligibility requirements. Individuals with higher incomes may not qualify for direct ROTH contributions, and deductibility rules for traditional IRAs can limit their effectiveness. LIRPs do not have income restrictions. Regardless of annual earnings or employment status, it is possible to fund a LIRP without eligibility concerns. As a result, LIRPs may be considered by high-net-worth individuals and those seeking alternative accumulation methods after retirement, or the ultimate estate building and wealth transfer vehicle.

Minimal Legislative Risk

Tax-advantaged accounts like ROTH IRAs represent a significant cost to the government in terms of lost tax revenue, making them potential targets for future legislative change.

LIRPs, on the other hand, have a history of resilience in the face of tax law reform. When Congress has adjusted the rules governing life insurance policies (notably in 1982, 1984, and 1988), existing policies have consistently been 'grandfathered' in under the old laws. This means owners of LIRPs have enjoyed protection from adverse changes affecting new buyers. Even under the scrutiny of the President's Advisory Panel on Federal Tax Reform in 2005, recommendations to change the tax treatment of life insurance policies ultimately preserved the advantages of pre-existing arrangements. (Do you really think that Congress will do something that will "kill" their own Golden Goose? Very doubtful.)

Grandfathering Of Existing Policies

The principle of grandfathering ensures that changes to tax law affecting life insurance policies do not retroactively impact the treatment of existing contracts. This provision allows policyholders to retain the original benefits of their Life Insurance Retirement Plans (LIRPs) even if new legislation changes rules for future policies. In an environment where lawmakers may seek new sources of tax revenue, grandfathering helps maintain consistency for current policyholders. So, get it while you can!

Provisional Income Exclusion

LIRPs are structured as permanent life insurance policies—such as Indexed Universal Life (IUL) or even "some" Whole Life policies that accumulate cash value either linked to market performance ***with*** downside protection or at a guaranteed minimum interest rate or both. These policies may offer returns comparable to other conservative investments, and the cash value has creditor protection.

Further, the proceeds from a LIRP do not, will not, affect your tax situation or trigger "provisional income" taxes on your Social Security Benefits.

So, the combination of asset growth, protection, and tax-free withdrawals and enhanced Living Benefits (think LTC) is a factor in why most high-net-worth individuals incorporate LIRPs into their retirement planning.

Flexible Access To Cash Value

LIRPs offer greater flexibility in accessing accumulated cash than many traditional retirement accounts. You can take policy loans or withdrawals at any time, for any reason, without penalty, provided the policy is properly structured and remains in force. There are no required minimum distributions (RMDs) and no age-based withdrawal rules, allowing you to tailor your retirement income to your actual needs rather than the dictates of the tax code.

Additional Living Benefits

This feature alone is beyond amazing in my opinion, and why ***"if you can qualify"*** makes this the hands-down champion of retirement planning without a doubt.

Most modern LIRPs offer "living benefits" such as accelerated death benefits for chronic or terminal illness, and long-term care like riders. These are other features that can provide financial support in the event of unexpected health challenges. Providing you have a doctor sign off that you cannot perform 2 of the 6 activities of daily living routines, (ADLs) or have been projected to pass away within 18 months, you would qualify. Features like these add another layer of protection and utility to the policy, making it much, much more than a simple tax-free accumulation vehicle.

EXAMPLE

You have a $700,000 IRA, and receive a pension of $22,000 per year, and Social Security benefits amounting to $17,000 annually. Your spouse was not employed outside the home and did not participate in a retirement program. You turned 66 and experienced a stroke, you became unable to care for yourself, and now require long-term care in a nursing home. You do not have a long-term care policy. How are you going to pay the $10,000 to $20,000 per month? ***Which of your assets are you going to sell first?***

WHAT ABOUT THE "STATE OR GOVERNMENT" TO TAKE CARE OF ME?

Before Medicaid (the government's medical assistance program) provides ***any*** coverage, you are required to undergo a "spend down." This process involves using ***all qualified assets*** and available savings and investments in your name (such as an IRA) to cover the cost of care. Additionally, portions of your pension and Social Security benefits ***must be*** allocated toward the long-term care expenses. Jointly held assets must also be reduced to $120,900 before Medicaid will begin covering the costs. **WHAT?** Yup, that's the law!

After your stroke and transfer to a long-term care facility, your wife becomes a "community spouse." In this situation, ***her*** retirement accounts are protected from spend down. However, she most likely does not have any retirement accounts, as she was a stay-at-home spouse and relies upon your IRA, pension, and Social Security benefits for retirement income.

Sad, but it would probably be best for the family financially if you were to pass away. Whoa, that's a lot - but true. If you passed away, in this instance, your wife would become the beneficiary of your pension, Social Security benefits, and a $700,000 IRA. Obviously, she would be very saddened that you were gone, but her life would continue pretty much unchanged financially. This would provide continued financial support for her.

However, since your stroke has led to long-term care needs, most of your assets may be required to be reallocated in advance to cover those upcoming expenses. Your wife is allowed to keep: one house, one car, $120,900 in cash, and a Minimum Monthly Maintenance Needs Allowance (MMMNA). At this time, it is $2,643.75 total per month. That's it. No Social Security, no pension, no IRA. Oh, and she still needs to pay utilities, property taxes, HOA fees, and homeowners' insurance, all on $2,643.75 per month. That's assuming your house is paid for, too!

The only way around this is "Medicaid Planning," in short, you must have repositioned or given away your assets ***60 months before*** you plan to file for Medicaid.

Let Me Give You Another Example. The LIRP Example.

Let's assume you are the same 66-year-old and have had your LIRP since you were 60. You have a "Death Benefit" of 4 million dollars. Your accumulated cash value is $800,000 from IRA conversions and other repositioned taxable accounts. You stopped contributing to the LIRP when you turned 66. You haven't accessed any of the cash value, and no need for RMDs as we've covered before. Unfortunately, you have inoperable cancer, or a stroke, Alzheimer's, or Dementia, or some other terrible illness you contract. You now need long-term care nursing, and you do not have a long-term care (LTC) policy.

With a LIRP, you can access a portion of the Death Benefit while you're still alive to cover your medical expenses! In most cases, up to 40% to 50% of the policy. In this case, 1 million dollars tax-free to help in your time of need. Notice I did not say your cash value. Let's assume your medical care is $20,000 per month. You live 14 months more. That's $280,000. Round that up to $300,000 for other various expenses. How long can you, and how comfortable are you, writing a check for that every month? Remember, Medicare WILL NOT COVER THAT, and you definitely do not want Medicaid.

Now, 14 months later, you have unfortunately passed away. Your beneficiary now receives $700,000 of the $1,000,000 you took for medical expenses, $3,000,000 more from your death benefit, and $800,000 in your cash value account. ALL WITHIN 30 DAYS - TAX FREE – PROBATE FREE – IN CASH! The best part is that no other assets were touched, used, or leveraged.

Show me another retirement plan that can do that!

Comparing LIRPs To Traditional Retirement Vehicles

The advantages of LIRPs become even clearer when compared side-by-side with traditional retirement tools:

Feature	LIRP	Roth IRA	Traditional IRA/401(k)
Tax-free distributions	Yes	Yes	No
Contribution limits	No	Yes	Yes
Income limits	No	Yes	No
Required minimum distributions	No	No	Yes
Impact on Social Security taxation	No	Yes	Yes
Asset protection	Yes	No	No
Access to living benefits	Yes	No	No
Legislative risk	No	Potentially High	High

Considerations And Potential Drawbacks

No financial strategy is without its drawbacks, and LIRPs do have some considerations that must be weighed:

- LIRPS may require ongoing premiums to keep the policy in force, which may be higher than traditional retirement account contributions. This is true if you do not correctly fund the plan well in the first 6 – 10 years. Structured correctly, you can usually stop after the 7th - 10th year if you wish.

- The policy must be structured carefully to avoid becoming a Modified Endowment Contract (MEC), which would result in less favorable tax treatment. A qualified representative can make sure that doesn't happen.
- Fees and insurance costs can have an impact on long-term cash value growth, so it is crucial to choose a well-designed policy from a reputable provider. This is correct, and it is the main thing that Brokers like to throw out to dissuade clients from implementing this plan. However, the "fees" they reference generally disappear within the first 3-5 years. Does the Broker's? Ask the Broker about their ongoing fees and commissions, whether the market goes up or down, and whether they provide tax-free living benefits and a tax-free, probate-free death benefit. You want to pay these fees up front as they solidify and pay for the guarantees the policy provides for your life and retirement.
- The biggest consideration is that you do have to qualify health-wise. It is a Life Insurance product, so not everyone gets approved. But if you do get approved, purchase as much as you can because, besides health considerations, it also goes by your age. Consult an agent as soon as you can. Because you're never as healthy and as young as you are right now.

My Review

The Life Insurance Retirement Plan (LIRP) is acknowledged as an effective, strategic, and flexible method for generating tax-free retirement income, subject to you being able to qualify for the policy.

It offers benefits such as tax-free distributions, no contribution or income limits, protection from future legislation we know will be coming, and additional living advantages.

LIRPs can serve as a critical part of a holistic financial plan, especially when traditional retirement solutions prove inadequate. For those looking to optimize asset growth, minimize tax exposure, and preserve their estate, the LIRP merits careful consideration within a diversified retirement portfolio.

Past conventional thinking was securing the highest possible life insurance coverage for the lowest necessary premium. In contrast, the LIRP approach involves acquiring only the insurance required under IRS regulations while funding the policy up to maximum allowable limits.

Please note that this is for one person. If you are married or plan to be (because no one knows who will become sick or die when), it is advisable to consider a LIRP for both people.

Let me even simplify it more. Between now and when you choose to retire, only one of three things will happen to you.

1. You die. Yup, that could happen. In which case, the money you had planned to have for your family in the future is there for them, tax-free, probate-free, in cash within 30 days. They'll miss you, but they'll be ok financially.
2. You become very sick, have a stroke, or are permanently disabled. You can't work anymore. You need a lot of medical attention and skilled nursing care. Remember, Medicare and regular health insurance will not cover these expenses for longer than 90 days. YOU will have to pay out of pocket for these expenses. How long can you write a check for $10,000 - $20,000 per month? How long do you want to? ***(Would you rather have "someone else" pay for it? Of course you would. Think the LIRP)***

3. You live! **<u>YAY</u>**, you made it! Best of all, you can now access your Social Security Benefits, and your cash in your LIRP retirement account, TAX FREE, and NOT pay income or provisional income tax. You access all the money you had deposited before and all the growth! ***You can do as you please for income from the LIRP. Either a monthly, quarterly, or annual check to you in equal amounts, or whatever you need. Tax-Free!*** Remember also, unlike an IRA or ROTH, you can access this anytime you need money. You do not have to wait until you're 59 1/2. It's your money. Furthermore, this is by far the best and most efficient way to build and transfer wealth to beneficiaries. How have all these very wealthy families transferred wealth, not paid inheritance tax, and have tax-free incomes, and for how many generations have they? Look up The Rockefeller Method.

So Why Hasn't Your CPA, Broker, Or Financial Advisor Told You About This Retirement Vehicle?

1. It's important to remember that the financial strategies of the wealthy often take time to be recognized, understood, and assimilated by even a CPA before they recommend it to their clients. Many CPA's do not understand all the benefits of a LIRP. Most are not licensed to.
2. Your securities advisor may have heard about it... But since they don't get a *commission for life* like they do with "securities," they won't. Why, because their Broker Dealer won't allow them to offer it. It takes away from their AUM (Assets Under Management) totals, of which they get a percentage every month.

If your advisor tries to tell you it is a ***"bad investment"***, remember they may have a hidden agenda (their income); they do not want to admit that it's a great program, or won't admit it, or they don't understand it.

Better yet, ask them if they'll pay for all of your future medical needs tax-free and provide a completely tax-free income, or a tax-free death benefit worth more than all the deposits you've made.

They won't. I've asked them, in person, while sitting there with their client, who became mine after that exchange. Again, it's not an "investment" either. It's a LIRP.

But, if it were truly a "bad investment" ..., **do you really think that the wealthiest 25% of people in the United States would own almost 50% of all of the insurance face amounts? Hmmmm**

I am not saying "do not have stocks, bonds, or mutual funds." I'm more advocating that if you're 50-60 years old, you should shift the majority of your portfolio away from market-based products for protection and peace of mind. If there is a major drop in your portfolio, you do not have the time to earn it again, and I assume you don't want to either.

Further, I am also an advocate for perhaps purchasing "Alternative" or non-conventional assets. Maybe some Crypto, maybe structured settlements, perhaps some RIETS and other real estate-backed programs. Just not the majority of your money. Money that you are comfortable with the risk. Only you can answer that. Explore the options with eyes wide open and a curious nature. Ask all the questions. Expect the best, but beware that there may also be the "worst".

Long Term Care Insurance

I want to mention a little about Long Term Care Insurance in its purest form. Long-term care insurance is available. Expensive, but available. After all, it's about making sure you're taken care of ***if*** the day comes when you can't do all the everyday things on your own. Such as cooking, getting dressed, going to the bathroom, bathing, or moving around safely.

Instead of relying only on family or draining your estate and finances, this type of insurance helps cover the cost of care. Whether that's in your home, an assisted living facility, or a nursing home. Think of it as peace of mind: it gives you choices, protects your retirement money, and eases the burden on your loved ones so they can focus on being there for you, not just caring for you.

You do have to qualify through a medically underwritten policy. It's not cheap, but it's cheaper than paying for it out of your own pocket if needed. However, if you do not use it, you most often lose all the funds you've spent on it over the years. LIRP will accomplish all of this with no additional costs, and you could have a higher monthly payout than the LTC policy.

Here are a few nationwide average monthly premium examples (for people around age 55–65) to give a sense of what people might pay:

- A 55-year-old man with level benefits approximately: ~$195/month
- A 55-year-old woman in similar policy approximately: ~$308/month
- A couple, both 65, combined policy approximately: ~$896/month

These are the main drivers of LTC insurance costs:

1. **Age at purchase** — Buying younger means lower premiums. The older you are, the more likely you are to need benefits, which raises costs.

2. **Gender / Life expectancy** – Women often pay more because they tend to live longer on average, so there's a greater chance benefits will be needed.
3. **Health status / Underwriting** – If you're in good health, a non-smoker, with a clean medical history, you'll pay less. Medical exams or questionnaire results matter.
4. **Benefit amount / Duration** – How much daily benefit you want, how many years or "benefit period" you want, whether you want coverage for home care + facility care, etc.
5. **Inflation Protection** – This adds significantly. A modest rider that increases the benefit amount annually (to keep up with inflation) can double or more than double the premium over a level benefit policy.
6. **Elimination / Waiting Period** – How long you have to wait after needing care before benefits begin. You can usually choose. A 90-day waiting period will cost less than a 0-day or 30-day waiting period, all else being equal.
7. **Location** – Costs differ quite a lot from state to state (and even county to county) due to the cost of care, wages, regulations, and the risk pool in that area.

There are some types of asset-based long-term care programs available that can convert annuities with riders to a substantial Long-Term Care benefit. Speak to a qualified advisor for more details.

The need for either a "living benefit" from a LIRP or a long-term care policy is paramount. Ask yourself this question before you become sick or disabled: ***"If you or your spouse becomes disabled, needs skilled nursing care, or has to go to a care facility, which of your current assets will you liquidate first?"***

Remember, it may cost as much as $10,000 or more every month - each!

As of this writing, there are now brokers, fiduciary advisors, and life agents who the families of deceased clients are suing. Why, because the "advisors" may have protected the client's money but did not look out for the "best interest" of the estate and the surviving spouse and family with long-term care need products. Many families lost their homes and nest eggs to the ravages of unforeseen medical expenses.

We will address this issue more as we progress through the book. Stay tuned!

Chapter SIX

PROBLEM SOLVING

> *You may delay... but time will not!*
>
> *- Benjamin Franklin*

Let's look at some real-world solutions to what may be a stumbling block for you. You're trying your best to get to the ZERO tax bracket in retirement and create peace of mind, with tax-free income and tax-free long-term care type of benefits in your retirement. Hopefully, we're addressing all the potential "what ifs" in your retirement.

While I personally am a huge fan of the LIRP, the simple fact is that you may have "someone" chirping in your ear about the other old mantra of "Buy term insurance and invest the difference."

I've heard this from clients for 40 years. The biggest problems are 2-fold. One, the "difference" is that the money you invest is most likely going to go into market-driven products that are potentially subject to loss of principal and earnings. Even if this is successful, it will also create a larger tax consequence in the future. Two, Along with that fact, over 75% of the people who have tried that don't do it. Or if they do, they stop after a year or so.

The LIRP is automatically a savings and cash accumulation program. No thinking about what stocks or mutual funds to invest in, and "oh my gosh, the market just had a big correction". Not a concern for the LIRP. You never "risk" your principal or gains, as the money is linked to the index without directly being in it. And even if the market corrects by 50% or more, no worries. (Same with an FIA. Fixed Index Annuity that I will cover below.)

The great thing is that the LIRP has the tax-free income, tax-free living benefits, and tax-free death benefit as part of the whole program. Remember, you can access portions of the death benefit for a living benefit to help or cover medical expenses if need be. ***Your stock or mutual portfolio will not.*** You may be able to "borrow" against your portfolio from a bank or the Brokerage house, but why? You're just creating more expense and making it complicated.

However, the biggest potential problem here is that you may not qualify for the LIRP medically.

WHAT DO WE DO THEN?

Several potential action items, in my opinion. Firstly, maximize your contributions to a ROTH. Yes, it may not be as much as you hoped to shield from future taxes, but it's a start. Do it every year you can.

Second, ideally, if you are still working, most likely you have "write-offs" or various deductions to soften the tax blow at once, to roll existing IRAs into a ROTH. Preferably into a fixed or indexed annuity (FIA). A ROTH conversion is one of the biggest plays going on in the market today.

Most investors believe that taxes will and have to increase in the future. If you cannot see yourself paying the full hit of taxes all at once, perhaps do a portion each year so that it will not push you into a significantly higher tax bracket.

Another less popular option in the minds of some is to use the money in the IRA to pay the taxes due and be done with it all at once. You're going to pay tax at some point in the future. Why not now, when taxes are at their lowest in many years, and more than likely going up in the future? (Pssst... taxes are on sale now!)

I know, I get it. This may seem like a dumb thing to do. However, that's an impulsive reaction to a very logical situation. Think of it like "taxes ***are*** on sale!", and who doesn't like to pay less for something when they can? Literally everyone, for everything, especially taxes.

This is the same process for converting IRAs to either a ROTH or a LIRP. "Bite the bullet" now, as you "know the outcome". Hopefully, you still have some write-offs and deductions to help, or you can wait for an unknown outcome in the future and the potential regret that will come with that decision. Either decision, it is recommended to discuss with a CPA who understands what you are trying to accomplish. Paying the tax now is not the end of the world, but it can make a much brighter world for you ***tomorrow*** in your retirement.

There is another option. It's why I suggested a Fixed Indexed Annuity. FIA.

- Many fixed annuity insurance companies offer a "bonus" to reposition your funds with them. Anywhere from 5% to 10% on the entire amount. That alone could soften the tax sting a little for you.
- They also accumulate money in a tax-favored way. It would be treated and deferred like your existing IRA, but

without the market risk, or you can convert it to a ROTH FIA.

- A few companies offer a non-medical, enhanced, long-term care rider in one form or another. Personally, I used this for my own mother. We repositioned a $100,000 CD she had. The CD was creating a taxable event each year on the little bit of interest that she received. She didn't really need the money immediately, so we reallocated it. The insurance company we placed it with had a healthcare rider attached to it. It effectively turned her $100,000 deposit into a $300,000 benefit if she needed it for long-term care. My mother did not have long-term care insurance. Unfortunately, she did end up using it for that very purpose. All her other assets, including her house, ***were not affected***. Her funds in the annuity and the rider covered everything. When she ultimately passed away, some funds were left in the annuity, and then were dispersed to the beneficiaries.
- "I heard annuities have surrender charges". ***Usually, they do, and thank goodness they do!*** (By the way, don't bank CDs have surrender charges?) What do I mean? Well, the surrender charges do a couple of good things. They put in place the safeguards and guarantees for your account. Don't you want an account with guarantees? Like minimum rate guarantees, no loss of principal or previous year's earnings ever guarantees. Surrender charges make sure the insurance company stays in business to provide you with those guarantees. Insurance companies, by law, must back your account dollar for dollar with their own money. You put in $250,000 – they have to put $250,000 in a trust account for you! Actually, they are required by law to have $1.05 for every dollar you have on deposit with them. It's called The Legal Reserve. Furthermore, in 4 years

and 12 days, can you tell me the exact value of your stock portfolio? How about in 6 years and 42 days? The insurance company can tell you about the worst-case scenario for your account on any given day or year because of those guarantees. Your brokerage company cannot.

- Insurance Companies that offer "fixed" products handle your deposits in more conservative ways than insurers that offer variable products. You can opt to grow your money within the general investment fund of the insurance company that administers the program. Or participate in the indexing features, as explained in the LIRP. Indexing to an index like the S&P 500, but not directly "in the market". Because insurance companies are in the business of managing risk, these types of returns tend to be more conservative. But fair and very consistent with NO risk of principal or previous year's earnings. That's another **"ZERO"** knowing that **0%** of your principal and previous year's earnings will never be lost in a market downturn.

Suze Orman-The Road to Wealth

» ***How do I know if an index annuity is right for me?***

» **"If you don't want to take risk but still want to play the stock market, a good index annuity might be right for you."**

CHAPTER SIX

IS MY MONEY SAFE WITH A LIFE INSURANCE COMPANY?

There literally is no safer place for you to put your money than a life insurance company. It's safe to say that "It's the safest place allowed by law to accumulate and safeguard your money within."

The entire industry is built upon managing risk and long-term growth with guarantees. Let me further illustrate. If you win the lottery (hope so for you!) and you opt to take the payments over 20 years instead of the reduced lump sum, what happens? How does the lottery guarantee that?

They are required by law to purchase an annuity! Same if you win a lawsuit with a structured settlement payout to you. They are required by law to purchase an annuity from a fixed life insurance company. Insurance companies are the only companies that can legally guarantee a structured payout.

The US life insurance companies alone have more assets and money than ***all*** the oil companies in the world combined! Think about that for a minute. It is scary to think about it, but the biggest insurance companies in the world aren't even located in the USA; they are in Europe! The industry overall is hundreds of years old, and trillions upon trillions of dollars in cash and assets. One insurance company I know has over $11 trillion in cash reserves alone. So yes, your money is more than safe. It's by far safer than any bank, anywhere. That's a whole different book I may write about later if you like this one.

Every insurance company is subject to incredible oversight and regulations. Every company is required to have "on hand" enough cash to cover any claims that are made upon them and even required to have "reinsurance". That is to have a specialized insurance company, to insure them! Yes, even Property and Casualty Insurance companies have reinsurance on them. (Warren Buffett owns 2 reinsurance companies.)

So, if you cannot qualify for a LIRP, but still want growth, protection of your account, and "some" long-term care features, a good Indexed Annuity might be perfect for your ROTH conversion or IRA rollover.

Another question I get is, "Ok, I still work, and I have an active 401(k) that both my employer and I contribute to. What's your suggestion?"

Wonderful, I say! Two things, first, continue with the contributions to the active 401(k). Maximize what you need to do to fully receive the employer's contribution. You then only contribute what you need to for that "free" money match. Take the rest of the money you normally would have put in your 401(k) and purchase a ROTH outside of the company plan.

Second, ask your HR/Benefits division if you're vested enough to roll out some of your 401(k) to a separate IRA you control. Then, in my opinion, see if you qualify to create a LIRP. If so, follow the conversion information I shared above to fund the LIRP and the excess dollars you were putting into the 401(k), now divert to your LIRP. Then, when you retire or if you change companies, roll the money into your LIRP then. If you cannot qualify for a LIRP, roll into a ROTH IRA that accepts monthly deposits.

Perhaps you want "some" cash available in an IRA, "just in case." Well, you can access an IRA after 59 1/2, and yes, you will be taxed. However, all is not gloomy. The IRS allows a married couple that files jointly a $30,700 standard deduction for 2025. So, keep great records, and with that deduction, providing you do not file an itemized return, you won't pay tax. Just because you can take money, doesn't mean you should. Remember that any amount you withdraw will count as "provisional income" and that adds to your income totals. Most likely, this will affect your Social Security Benefits.

If your Social Security is tax-free now, it may create a taxable problem you don't want. However, some people use this as a way to help liquidate their IRAs for conversion and placement.

Another question sometimes asked is, "I have or will have a pension when I retire, what's the outcome then?"

If your pension is higher than the $30,700 threshold in 2025, that means up to 50% of your Social Security benefits could be subject to taxation at your highest marginal rate. But remember, the focus should always be on what you can control, rather than worrying about things outside your influence.

Bad news is that reaching the 0% tax bracket with a pension is simply 99% not possible. Your pension alone uses up your deductions, which means any additional income becomes taxable by default. This is one of the key risks associated with having a pension during retirement. In such cases, it's wise to turn our attention to your other liquid assets, as these still present opportunities to manage their tax impact in the future. (Psst... taxes are on sale now!)

To be proactive, if your expected pension does surpass $30,000, the main goal should be to keep the rest of your tax-deferred accounts at ZERO tax. Convert now to a ROTH or LIRP while you can, and hopefully still have some deductions to use.

Remember why: both your pension and half of your Social Security would count as "provisional income," which determines how much of your Social Security gets taxed. The more provisional income you have, the more likely a significant portion of your Social Security benefits will be taxed.

Effective, immediate, and future tax planning is crucial. So, what's the takeaway? If you're currently in the 22% federal tax bracket and have some room before hitting the 24% bracket, it's wise to "bite the bullet." Move assets from your forever taxed, tax-deferred bucket to a tax-free, never taxed bucket, like through a Roth conversion or a LIRP if your circumstances allow.

If you unlock your tax-deferred funds at a 22% rate and apply deductions, you may save more compared to waiting and potentially facing rates of 30–40% or more. You could be missing a valuable opportunity. Waiting until 2026, 2027, or the election year of 2028 or even later could mean facing much higher tax rates. This would, of course, lead to regret for not acting when rates were historically low. Potentially placing you in a higher tax bracket than you might anticipate.

Chapter SEVEN

A DIFFERENT KIND OF ZERO

> *At its best, life is completely unpredictable.*
>
> *– Christopher Walkin*

I truly hope by now you're becoming a fan of **ZERO**. My goal is that the information I've shared so far is resonating with you and inspiring you to develop a new plan of action for your retirement. Nothing would give me greater pleasure than knowing the book has helped you understand retirement options better, paying attention to the potential pitfalls we've been discussing, and, most importantly, taking action. My email address will be listed at the end of the book; feel free to drop me a line.

I need to now cover a different topic. It may be something you "think" you know about, or you are already prejudiced about, but shouldn't be, in my opinion. Heck, it may not even apply to your situation. But it might be for your "unknown" future or someone you know. So here we go.

I will approach this in several different ways. I think you'll see the need for this for many seniors as we go along. The effort, time, and money you've dedicated to getting to the **ZERO** tax bracket are wonderful and will change your retired life forever, so let's make sure we keep it.

What if you still have a mortgage on your home and are still making monthly payments? That's less money for you to enjoy your retirement. Time and money go traveling, dining at amazing restaurants with your spouse, and with family and friends. At this stage of your life, you've earned the right to be a little selfish and indulge in things you've always dreamt of once in a while. Don't be reckless, of course, but do experience new and different things. Do the things you always promised yourself or your spouse. Now you can!

In this case, if you do not own your home outright, you may have significant other debt. Like credit cards, car loans, boat loans, whatever. These can be a drag on your retirement, your mindset, and your emotions. It's not what you worked so hard for all your life, is it?

Even if you own your home outright, you still need to keep it maintained, keep property taxes current, Homeowners Insurance current, and if you have HOA dues, you must keep that current as well. These "costs" are often more than many seniors in retirement had figured on, especially surprise "assessments".

Maybe you want to or need to remodel or make changes to be able to live more comfortably. Wheelchair ramp, wider doorways, lower counters, step-in shower/bathtubs. Yard remodel and maintenance. These all cost money. Maybe money you didn't count on.

Perhaps you opted not to pursue the ROTH or LIRP plans, and now you're faced with pulling money from your retirement dollars, most likely an IRA, and subject to a lot more tax than you anticipated. And God help you if the tax laws have changed.... You get where I'm going here.

Almost every senior citizen I have ever spoken with, in 35 different states, and 30-plus years of working with retirees and pre-retirees, say the same thing. Their goal or wish is to remain in their home until they are "carried out." Admirable goal, I feel. Why not? It's where they are most comfortable and have spent most of their lives there, most likely.

But, if they don't have a LIRP, or Long-term care insurance, and become sick, hurt, or disabled, they will need to pay for Skilled Nursing, and Home Healthcare out of their own savings. When that money runs out, you'll still need to be taken care of. Medicaid most likely would step in, and then the State could put a lien on your home. Even if it's in a Trust. It's part of "The State Recovery Act."

You see, the other thing the majority of all those thousands of seniors I've worked with have said... They NEVER want to leave their house to the STATE! They all would like to pass it on to their children, the church, or a charity. NOT THE STATE. But without proper planning, that is a very real outcome.

How do I know? When I was in college, my stepfather's mother became a "ward of the state" in Nebraska. She had Dementia and lived a very long time with it, as most patients with that disease do. Bottom line was they lost the family farm that had been in the family for over 100 years at that time. No legacy to continue or leave. Thousands of memories and stories are gone forever. No more family farm.

Part of the reason I feel that I have been so successful in this industry is that I truly do look for all the "what ifs" that people could face. This has been another one.

Now Let's Get To The Next ZERO

Now, because of the things we've covered before, rising living costs, unexpected home maintenance, medical expenses, and changes in tax laws can quickly erode decades of savings.

Owning a home is often the largest asset for most retirees. As financial landscapes shift, many retirees seek ways to leverage the equity in their homes to enhance their quality of life and maintain their independence. One increasingly popular solution is the reverse mortgage, which, under current laws, offers distinct benefits tailored for today's retirees.

What Is A Reverse Mortgage?

A reverse mortgage is a loan available to homeowners aged 62 and older that allows them to convert part of the equity in their homes into tax-free cash. Unlike traditional mortgages, where borrowers make monthly payments to the lender, a reverse mortgage pays the homeowner. The loan is then repaid when the owner sells the house, moves out permanently, or passes away. The most common type of reverse mortgage is the Home Equity Conversion Mortgage (HECM), which is insured by the Federal Housing Administration (FHA). Current laws provide great consumer protection and flexibility, making reverse mortgages a viable and secure financial tool for seniors.

I Want To Leave The House For The Children

That's a noble and wonderful sentiment. One that I hear from every client I've ever worked with. Just a couple of things to think about. Do you really think the children will want to move back into their old home? What if there are 2 or more children and they are married, with their own children? (Believe it or not, I've had people think that would happen.) But let's get back to the potential of "if" one or both of you need long-term care. The State will be first in line if you do not have the means to fund your own level of care. More on this later on.

Key Benefits Of A Reverse Mortgage

1. *Supplementing Retirement Income*

One of the principal advantages of a reverse mortgage is the ability to supplement retirement income. Social Security, pensions, and retirement accounts may not always be sufficient, especially as healthcare, insurance, and day-to-day living costs rise. A reverse mortgage allows seniors to access the equity tied up in their homes without having to sell or downsize, or provide a steady stream of funds to cover expenses or enjoy retirement. Payments can be received as a lump sum, monthly disbursements, a line of credit, or a combination, offering flexibility to match individual financial needs tax-free. (Think **ZERO** in action again!)

2. *No Monthly Mortgage Payments Required*

With a reverse mortgage, homeowners are not required to make monthly loan payments. This can provide significant relief for those on fixed incomes, eliminating one of the largest recurring expenses in retirement. Instead, loan repayment is deferred until the home is no longer the borrower's primary residence. Seniors must still pay property taxes, homeowners' insurance, and maintain the property, plus any HOA Fees, but the absence of mortgage payments frees up cash flow for other priorities.

3. *Staying in Your Home*

Current laws ensure that borrowers can remain in their homes as long as they meet the loan requirements. This aligns with the wishes of most seniors who prefer aging in place, surrounded by familiar environments and memories. Unlike selling the home to access equity, or a 2nd mortgage, a reverse mortgage allows continued occupancy ***without*** the financial pressure to relocate or adding monthly debt.

4. *Federally Backed Consumer Protections*

The HECM program, backed by the FHA, includes several consumer protections:

- Mandatory Counseling: Borrowers must attend HUD-approved counseling sessions to ensure they fully understand the terms, costs, and responsibilities of a reverse mortgage.
- Non-Recourse Loan: The homeowner (or their heirs) will never owe more than the home's value at the time of sale. If the loan balance exceeds the property value, FHA insurance covers the difference.
- Spousal Protections: Under current regulations, eligible non-borrowing spouses can remain in the home after the borrower passes away, provided requirements are met, like insurance is active, the property taxes and HOA dues are current, and, of course, maintenance of the home is maintained.
- Limits on Fees and Interest Rates: There are caps on origination fees and interest rates, making the loans more affordable and transparent.

5. *Flexible Payment Options*

Reverse mortgages offer several payment methods, including lump-sum payments to you, monthly advances, and lines of credit that can be accessed as needed. All tax-free! The line of credit option is especially popular, as unused funds grow over time and provide a safety net for future needs such as medical emergencies or unexpected repairs.

6. *Tax-Free Proceeds*

Funds received from a reverse mortgage are considered loan advances, not income, and are therefore not subject to federal income tax. This provides retirees with additional resources without increasing their tax burden, which is crucial when withdrawals from retirement accounts like IRAs or 401(k)s can trigger significant tax liabilities. Also, it is NOT counted as Provisional Income affecting Social Security Benefits.

7. *Long-Term Care and Healthcare Planning*

Many seniors face the challenge of paying for long-term care, home healthcare, or adapting their homes for accessibility. The proceeds from a reverse mortgage can be used to finance home modifications, skilled nursing care, or other medical expenses, helping retirees maintain autonomy and comfort without depleting other savings or assets.

8. *Legacy Planning and Estate Preservation*

Current laws provide that heirs may repay the reverse mortgage and retain the property or sell the home and keep any equity remaining after the loan is satisfied. Just like a regular loan you may have had before. Because a reverse mortgage is a non-recourse loan, heirs are protected from any deficiency if the home's value falls below the loan balance. This allows many families to preserve some legacy, with clear guidelines for estate settlement. Heirs usually have at least 6 months after the last spouse leaves the home.

9. *Protection Against Market Downturns*

This is a great feature. Unlike home equity lines of credit (HELOCs) or other loans, reverse mortgages cannot be canceled or reduced due to market fluctuations or changes in the borrower's income or credit. Once established, the terms are secure, giving retirees confidence in their financial planning regardless of economic uncertainty.

Eligibility And Requirements Under Current Laws

To qualify for a HECM reverse mortgage, applicants must:

- Being 62 or older, A legal spouse, non-borrowing, even many years younger, may live in the home until they choose to leave, even if the older, borrowing spouse passes away. The older you are, the more money you have access to.
- Live in the home as their primary residence; No, you cannot rent your home out on this program. All bills, utilities, and insurances have to be in your name and attached to that address. Yes, they actually do check and have the right to.
- Own the home outright or have a low mortgage balance that can be paid off with reverse mortgage proceeds. Then, there are no more future mortgage payments.
- Demonstrate the ability to pay ongoing property charges such as taxes, insurance, and maintenance.
- Participate in a HUD-approved counseling session before application.
- Credit and income are not determining factors for this program.

Eligible properties include single-family homes, FHA-approved condominiums, and some multi-unit properties.

You can also use a Reverse Mortgage to purchase a home. After the required down payment, the HUD-approved lender would cover the balance of the purchase, and, subject to you keeping insurance, taxes, and maintenance up to date, the home is yours with no more future payments!

Potential Considerations And Drawbacks

While reverse mortgages offer considerable benefits, it's important to consider all aspects:

- Costs and Fees: Upfront mortgage insurance premiums, closing costs, and servicing fees may apply just like a regular loan.
- Reduction in Home Equity: As loan funds are drawn, home equity decreases, leaving less for heirs or future needs.
- Ongoing Obligations: Failing to keep up with property taxes, insurance, or maintenance can trigger default and foreclosure.
- Impact on Public Assistance: Proceeds may affect eligibility for Medicaid or Supplemental Security Income (SSI), but not Social Security or Medicare.

Consulting with financial advisors and thoroughly reviewing all documentation is essential before making a decision.

There is another thought to this program that is not often spoken of. If you withdrew the majority of the money out of the home as a reverse mortgage, and have safeguarded it properly, with proper planning, you most likely could go on Medicaid if needed and not be as frustrated if the State liens your home, as you now have the majority share of equity out of it!

Conclusion: Empowering Retirement With Modern Reverse Mortgages

Reverse mortgages, under current laws, have evolved into safe, flexible instruments designed to help seniors unlock the value of their homes while protecting their interests and legacy. With robust federal oversight, improved consumer safeguards, and options tailored to individual circumstances, a reverse mortgage can empower retirees to maintain independence, supplement income, and manage unexpected expenses—all while remaining in the comfort of their own homes. Thoughtful planning, professional guidance, and careful consideration ensure that seniors can leverage this important tool for a more secure and enjoyable retirement.

Further, you can use the funds for pretty much anything you'd like to. How about a magnificent dream trip, a new RV, funding the children's or grandchildren's college programs, or helping them buy a house? Or ... to pay taxes for an IRA rollover to a ROTH or LIRP! The Death Benefit of the LIRP alone will more than cover the reverse mortgage home loan for the children and still provide much more cash they'll ultimately inherit, again tax-free! It's a great option for most.

Chapter EIGHT

I JUST WANNA GO FISHING

> *Beware of little losses... a small leak can still sink a great ship!*
>
> *- Benjamin Franklin*

The focus of this book, as you know, is adjusting your mindset and your retirement and investment portfolio to a ZERO tax, tax-free distribution in retirement. It is not easy, but it's also not impossible. Taking advantage of new products that are available to consumers now, and being disciplined enough to implement them.

I've been blessed to meet and work with so many people of all ages in the 30-plus years I've been doing this work for seniors, and smart 40-50 years olds working hard on preserving their nest eggs the right way. So many different areas of planning that I could write 10 books about them. I want to share one more important story with you, though.

The title of this chapter, "I just wanna go fishing," actually came from a client of mine, several years ago, when he was about to retire after 30 years of service, working for the State of California. His name is Bob. Heck of a nice guy to work with. This is a 100% true story as it actually unfolded.

I want to share his story because so many pre-retirees were and are in the same situation. After Bob and I spoke via the phone a couple of times. Then, after listening to what he was looking to do for his optimal retirement plan, I said, "Come on down and please bring in your statements of your accounts so we can begin to understand what we are working with." Bob agreed, and we scheduled the appointment.

He arrived 4 days later with a good-sized stack of papers. Bob began laying out all the statements all over the conference table. Statement after statement of no less than 4 brokerage companies, banks, and a credit union. He had the last 3 months of each account in descending order. I can still see it in my mind. So organized and laid out so nicely, and he was quite proud of it.

So, I asked Bob, "This is great. Why do you have so many different accounts?" His answer to him made complete sense. "Well, Lance, I was always told I needed to diversify."

I took a few minutes and reviewed each stack, carefully noting how long he had been in each one, and then reviewed the makeup of the stocks and mutual funds he also had. I said, "Bob, you're right that you need to diversify your investments and portfolio. But you own almost the same thing in each brokerage company. Bob, we diversify so that if one sector takes a downturn, it doesn't affect the rest of the portfolio. With almost the same type of products and funds in each brokerage company, you could be in trouble if "that" sector has a big adjustment. You need to diversify your selections of products, not just brokerage companies!"

Poor Bob was so proud of what he had created, saved, and invested for so long, but didn't see or understand the inherent bigger picture at risk. Keep this in mind as I share more about Bob.

Bob was a very handy guy. Built his own garage, remodeled his house, extended his patio; you get the idea. Bob also loves the outdoors. He purchased an acre of land on a lake up in The Sierra Mountains. His dream is to have his "get away" and retirement escape.

He loves fishing and "getting away from it all." He ended up building his own cabin up there. He was way off the grid, no power, plumbing, etc. Hooked a generator up, ran wires throughout the cabin, etc. You get the idea. Every chance he could, he would be up at the cabin.

Most relevant to our story is that there was absolutely no TV or cell phone service. Bob would go up there for weeks at a time. No outside contact at all, and he loves it.

Unfortunately, there was a slight correction in the market shortly after we met. Fortunately, Bob was home and took care of everything without much loss. What I had told him about, and what my concern was, did, in fact, happen. All his accounts took a little hit. He called me again and came to see me with his newly updated statements.

Let me ask ***you*** the same question I asked Bob at that appointment. "Bob, let's assume you have a phenomenal performance in your portfolio. 35% to 45% gain! Wow! Is that big gain going to change your life, really? Cause you to buy a bigger house, or flashier new car, or new designer clothes?" He laughed and said, "No, that it wouldn't really affect him or change his life at all. He'd just be happy and feel good about more money in his account."

"Great," I said, "Now, how about if there is a prolonged downturn in the market. Say a 35% to 45% loss. Think about 2008. Would that affect you?" He stopped and said, "Yes, it definitely would." It would mean careful budgeting of certain things, such as trips and gas for his truck. Potentially even delay his full retirement for a while.

I said to Bob, "***There are 3 phases of money***. The accumulation phase, the preservation phase, and the distribution phase. You've already accumulated most of what you're going to. You're needing to now preserve what you have as you don't want to go back and make it all over again, do you?"

"No," he said. "Then we have to create a plan for the best and most efficient way to avoid risk for the preservation of your hard-earned money, and the best and most efficient way to distribute the money to you and or your heirs."

I then said, "Bob, what would happen to your money if you are up at the cabin fishing, and there is a bigger correction, and you didn't even find out about it until you're back a week or so later, and it's too late".

Bob sat there for a while, looking at his statements, shaking his head, taking in everything I said, and realizing he had too much "at risk". Potential gain against real potential loss did not sit well with him. Unfortunately, at that time, he had no solid plan for preservation or distribution on a "favored basis".

For several minutes, he just sat there shaking his head. He knew I was right about his plan. More money wouldn't make his life better, but less money would make it miserable, especially now that it just happened a little bit to him, and I have now made him aware of the "hole" in his plan.

He then looked up at me, shoved all the statements towards me, and said, "You deal with it. I just wanna go fishing." I said, "I'd be happy too, Bob". I then laid out a plan over the next several days for maximizing growth, safety, and minimizing taxes. Bob is very happy and finally got clarity, peace of mind, and comfort to go fishing wherever, whenever he wants to.

My hope for each of you is that by reading this book, you have clearly defined what you want for your retirement and have the ZERO strategy in place.

Obtain peace of mind and face each day knowing that this part of your life is dialed in and moving along nicely with no fear and no regrets.

Chapter NINE

10,000-FOOT OVERVIEW

> *"Loss's hurt you more than gains will ever, ever help you!"*

There has been a tremendous amount of information shared with you so far. I hope you've enjoyed my stories, and this book has triggered your mindset to begin a serious effort to safeguard your existing plan and portfolio. Remember, it's not about what you have, it's about what you keep.

The journey of a 1,000 miles begins with a single first step. So, in my opinion, "speaking as your future retirement," you really need to take your first steps, ***your*** journey, of what I've covered, before they change the laws. Restructure your traditional IRAs into ROTHs or in a LIRP if you haven't yet.

This book should be a blueprint of where and how to start looking. Remember, a properly structured ZERO tax retirement can transform your Social Security benefit to a ZERO tax benefit as well. You just cannot forget about the provisional tax, and if you earn too much, you do pay more tax.

The fact is that if your IRA income is taxed, more than likely your Social Security will also be taxed. Together, that can be financially and emotionally devastating! Between taxes on everything, you could deplete your nest egg 6 or 7 years sooner than you planned. Read that again slowly.

Now, factor in a medical scare for you or a spouse. You could be "cooked!" You may have to get a reverse mortgage just to cover living expenses.

I've seen some really sad stories. I can't tell you how many times people, after coming to see me speak, reached out to me - ***after*** they've had a problem or major setback. Kind of like closing the gate after the animals escaped. Not good, and in too many cases, I couldn't do anything to help.

It doesn't have to be that way. There is so much great planning that can be done to protect your future and your assets now. It may be uncomfortable, it may not be what you're used to, but it sure beats the alternative!

Emotions can be a sad but true reason that can derail your best-laid plans. You have to get into the logical side of your mind. Think of regrets you may have in other areas of your life from an inaction on something you didn't follow through on. This would be a lot larger for the rest of your retired life.

Finding and funding the correct programs to balance your retirement should be your priority after you finish this book. Begin research to see you through, and outline questions for solid planning for the "what ifs" that are inevitably going to come your way. How best to face them and pay for them? Am I comfortable if taxes increase significantly in the next 5 years? What if they reduce Social Security Benefits or Medicare? Are you prepared for that? There are so many unknowns, but hopefully I've brought them up to you in time to really realize potential shortfalls and take steps to safeguard yourself now in your existing plans.

You will need someone to help you with these steps. Someone who knows and understands the "pitfalls" ahead. Remember, most financial advisors and almost all brokers are the "wrong" choice. They focus on returns, diversification, accumulation and defer, defer, defer.

In other words, more taxes. You'll need someone who can speak the same language as what you have been reading. Make calls, interview them. ***If they don't sound like me and what you've been reading here... tell them to move on.*** Better still, if you're not having luck with that, reach out to us; either I or one of my associates will be happy to speak with you.

Again, folks, I'm NOT saying, don't have a portfolio of stocks, bonds, mutual funds, etc. What I am saying is, have your base, your retirement foundation, if you will, in safe non-risk accounts. What percentage of potential gain is worth the risk of potential significant losses?

It takes a 43% gain - just to get back "even" from a 30% loss!

Can you, will you, have time to recoup losses if there is any?

"Jim Cramer's Real Money"

» "If you want to retire at sixty, I would put more than half of your retirement money in **fixed income in your forties**. If you intend to work for years after sixty, I would put much less in those placeholders. **Your fifties begins the shift toward more fixed income**. And finally, in your sixties, unless, again, you keep working, fixed income should dominate. **Your opportunities to grow your money are now** limited, and the reward isn't worth the risk."

» "Only as you get closer to needing the money should your caution take hold so that **you don't let a lifetime's worth of savings be wiped out by a swift downturn in the market right before you need the money.**"

Chapter TEN

EXAMPLE RETIREMENT PLANS

> *The investor of today does not profit from yesterday's growth.*
>
> *- Warren Buffett*

I thought that it might be helpful to give you a few brief other examples we've done for clients in the past.

You met Bob in Chapter 8, and his realization to take the risk out of the money he couldn't afford to lose. To give him "peace of mind", asset protection, and the ability to convert to a permanent income he'd never outlive. He did keep some money (non-qualified) in one brokerage account to hopefully make a few extra dollars in the future, but not enough to risk his peace of mind - mindset.

Now Bob did have a pension that kicked in when he finally fully retired, so getting to the ZERO tax bracket wasn't an option. Too much money coming in every year from his Social Security and Pension. Further, he had a health condition that precluded him from obtaining a LIRP. So, we did a ROTH conversion of his 401(k) and other IRAs he had. We positioned into an FIA (fixed indexed annuity) with the LTC medical rider "in case" he needs LTC. We also managed to get him a small face amount "non-medically underwritten" 20-year term policy with a "return of premium" if not used. It was a smaller face amount, but enough to give his daughters to offset any taxes that may become due when he passes away. A very solid plan for Bob!

You heard me mention my mother. By repositioning her CD to the Fixed Annuity with the Long-Term Care rider, it was a solid option for her as she ended up using that product, and never had to touch any other assets to be able to live comfortably, at home with regular in-home Nursing care. She lived quite comfortably on her Social Security, and she had a few extra dollars coming in monthly from an annuity that was in a monthly payout mode. For her, it was like getting 2 paychecks every month. She was also happily married to a retired farmer for many years. They shared living expenses, so they were very comfortable and stress-free in retirement.

For these other specialized scenarios that we have done for clients, I will not break out every step, but rather give you the general outline of what was done. Know this, that in every case, reducing potential future tax obligations as outlined in the previous chapters was always done to the fullest extent we could.

LADDERING

We created "laddering" for some of our clients who were most comfortable with wanting a predictable income (paycheck) for years. In that case, I'd basically ask, "What was the amount of money per month you'd like coming in?" They gave me their number, so I requested the statements for where the pools of money were. I looked at it, did calculations, and said, "No problem. How about we give you a raise over that amount every few years, oh, ***and by the way, when we are done in 12 -15 years, you'll have close to the same amount of money we started with!"***

Wait... What? They were always beyond surprised to say the least, and of course, wanted to begin right away. This solution, called laddering or split ladder annuities, is again a specialized type of planning that is "out there" – you just need the right type of advisor to put it in place.

Life Insurance

Yes, I know I've covered this a lot. But here are some other creative ways to create wealth, make you more efficient, and create a lasting financial family legacy.

I've had many clients implement the following creative plans.

Many families are blessed to have accumulated significant money. Most of those clients want to divest some money from their estate year by year. Often, this is done by gifting money to one or more children according to the IRS guidelines. At this time, for 2025, both the husband and the wife can gift $19,000 from each parent to each child. Generally, there were 2-3 children. So up $38,000 to each child, without triggering the gift tax. (Yes, the IRS can tax gifts. Great news, huh?)

I said, "That's great, but what do they usually do with the gift money?" Most every time they responded with, "They spend it, because they know they will inherit a portion of the estate when we pass." I say, "How does that make you feel?" They usually are not enthused with what the children do with the money. They feel like they waste it. Because when they grew up, most of them only received money ***if*** they were out working for it and saving it. (I know I had to, did you?) Anyway, I said, "Sounds like they are money motivated, and you'd like them to have an understanding of how money works and what money can do. Is that correct?" They have always agreed. I said, "Let's teach them the power of leverage." Usually, they look very surprised at me. Let me explain, "Gift them what you planned, however instead of you giving them $38,000 – you give them $8,000 each and $30,000 per person goes to fund a Life Insurance Policy on you! They have an "insurable interest, so it makes sense" (Now we could do a last to die policy, or just on the father or just the mother, or both, whatever they chose.)

"The children will then split the Multimillion-dollar life policy. Over 10 years, they have put in only $300,000 each on average from their parents' gifting. They will then receive millions of dollars tax-free, probate-free, in cash, within 30 days – each! Oh, and if you become sick or disabled, instead of draining the assets in the estate, you can have a living benefit, tax-free, to fund your Long-Term Care needs! It's money you're going to "give away" (gift) anyway, so why not leverage it, teaching them that principle? Not a bad return for them as well!"

Over 90% of the clients I shared that concept with - LOVED IT!

One client sat his kids down and told them about it, and gave them the chance to opt out and keep the annual gift or go for the "bigger prize" as he called it at the end. All but one child did that. Boy, when the dad died, she (the daughter) was pissed off! Sure, she had quite a few new handbags, "cool" clothes, and a few great trips. But that fades quickly. Several clients did end up using the Living Benefits (LTC) feature, and everyone was grateful that other portions of the estate were not encumbered or drained.

I think it's a brilliant way to get funds out of the estate and grow the estate tax-free. Now, please note, the same could be done at much, much lower levels, say $10,000 a year. You get the picture.

The only thing better than that is if I show you how to get your premiums paid for by "someone" else. ***Really.*** Hold on because this is awesome.

CHAPTER TEN

PREMIUM FINANCING

These next 2 concepts are not available to 90% of the Financial Advisors out there. This is specialized planning we have been doing for years. So here we go.

If you are a self-employed businessperson, or a professional in some area that could deposit a minimum of $2,100 a month away ($25,000 a year) for 5 years... I have a way to get a bank to match that same amount each year in your account. Seriously! So, your $25,000 and the banks $25,000 = $50,000 a year in your retirement LIRP. After the 5th year, you stop contributing, and they will continue and put in $50,000 per year for up to the next 10 years! No kidding. You technically could put up to $50,000 a year in, and they match that amount. As I mentioned before, they will then put in $100,000 each year for up to the next 10 years!

Again, share this around. If you're a valued employee, a Realtor, a Doctor, a Dentist, or anyone Self-Employed who earns any amount of money and could contribute at least $12,000 to $25,000 per year, you've got the Golden Ticket here! The best self-directed Retirement Plan going.

Oh, and it also includes the tax-free Living Benefits rider for you (think LTC), too! Try to beat that with any Stock or mutual fund! No, it's not on margin. This is NOT an investment. It's a Fixed Life Insurance product.

You keep all the growth of the indexing over all those years at the indexing of that higher amount of money. Remember, NO loss of principal or gains ever!

Now, of course, the bank doesn't do it for free. They are charging a fair interest rate. One year after they stop depositing money in your account, the bank will withdraw their money and interest, usually in one withdrawal or over a couple of years.

You still have significantly more money than if you had just done it on your own deposits.

You keep everything else, including the death benefit and LTC benefits! This is singlehandedly one of the most amazing wealth accumulation and protection vehicles in the specialty market today. There is no risk in this, and the bank has no risk either. The policy itself is the collateral. If you pass away before completion, the bank receives its money and interest. Your beneficiaries receive your cash and the death benefit, tax-free, in cash, probate-free, within 30 days. It's amazing, isn't it!

PREMIUM FINANCING WEALTH TRANSFER

It keeps getting better! Remember earlier when I wrote about "gifting" money to your children? This is the same principle and program. Except that the money you deposit now is in each child's name, ***and*** the same money you put in, the bank matches it for 5 years. Then, in the next 10 years, the bank is the sole depositor.

So, 3 children? Then 3 plans. Same dollar amount you would have put in or "given away" anyway (gifting) – with ONE big difference. The children, after the 15th year, providing they are 21 or older (yes, you can start this very young), may access the cash for college, or buy a home, or let it ride for their retirement! $25,000 a year for 5 years at starting age 18, with the banks matching, is well over $5 million in tax-free cash at age 65! For only putting in for 5 years! ***Plus***, the death benefit, and the LTC rider! You have secured their financial future, eliminated debt and taxes, and addressed Long-Term Care concerns for your children! Oh, and since it's in a Life Insurance Policy, it is **NOT** subject to creditors now or in the future. (You can do these programs with as little as $12,000 per year in most cases)

I could go on and on, but you get the idea. I'm going to bet that a good majority of the concepts I have shared with you, you probably like. But perhaps you've never heard of them. WHY IS THAT? Is it that no Broker or financial advisor has shared these ideas with you? WHY?

There is so much available to help you, help yourself, and your family. You just need to take those first steps with the right people in your corner.

Believe it or not, several clients have created several gifting policies for each child. You see, after the 5th year, you do not make more deposits. So, you could start another policy for your child.

That's truly creating multigenerational tax-free wealth!

Chapter ELEVEN

OFTEN ASKED QUESTIONS

> ***The easiest way to double your money? - Fold it in half and put it in your pocket!***
>
> ***- Kim Hubbard***

The primary goal of this book is to stimulate you and guide you into taking action to begin safeguarding your hard-earned assets from the looming, menacing tax "freight train" that's bearing down on all of us. Remember, it's hard to get hit by a train if you're not on the tracks! (Pssst... taxes are on sale now!)

Hopefully, you re-read this book and refer back many times as continued inspiration for searching for your ideal strategy to better the next chapter in your life.

As emphasized throughout, the most effective strategy is to restructure your assets ***now*** from "forever taxed" to "never taxed!" Take all the steps you can to achieve a ZERO tax bracket in retirement. While the advantages and benefits of a ZERO tax bracket are clear, I do understand that the "journey" to get there can be tough and is potentially filled with challenges and unexpected pitfalls. Remember when I said, "Just because something is familiar doesn't make it right." Especially in these times.

I know writing a check now for taxes on a conversion isn't either familiar or comfortable. But you will be very glad you did when you are in retirement. (Yes, I expect a glowing review and update from you)

Because it is natural when you solve a problem to have more questions and some fear about what you're doing, below are some of the most common questions that usually come up.

For application and personalized advice tailored to your needs, I recommend working with a tax-free planning specialist, perhaps in tandem with a CPA who truly understands this model. As I've said before, it may not be the person you work with now.

First question I'd ask after they "pitch you" on how awesome they are is, "If the markets go down, could I lose principal and gains?" Next question, "Will my distributions affect my Social Security and Provisional Tax?" "Will your plan provide me a living benefit that's tax-free?" "Do I need to take RMDs?" You get the idea.

The LIRP (Life Insurance Retirement Plan)

Q: What kinds of expenses should I expect inside a LIRP?

A: Expenses in a LIRP primarily come from the cost of the life insurance portion of the policy. These costs are typically front-loaded, meaning they're higher in the first several years while the insurance company is covering the death benefit and establishing reserves. Over time, however, the cost of insurance decreases as your cash value grows, making the overall expense ratio much smaller compared to the early years.

When averaged over the life of the plan, costs usually fall in the 1%–1.5% range annually. That may sound similar to fees in mutual funds or a 401(k), but here's the difference: in most traditional investment accounts, you're paying advisor fees (1%–2%), mutual fund expense ratios, and often hidden costs like "loads" or internal trading fees.

With a LIRP, expenses are transparent and tend to decrease relative to your account value as it grows. In many cases, the lifetime costs of a properly designed LIRP are *less* than the fees investors pay in a traditional retirement account without realizing it.

Another thing to note: LIRPs don't charge capital gains taxes on growth. So, while you might pay a small percentage in insurance costs, you avoid an ongoing tax drag on your money. That's a trade many retirees are happy to make.

Q: When can I start accessing my money in a LIRP?

A: Access depends on the carrier and how the plan is structured, but most LIRPs include a "surrender period" during the first several years, where withdrawals may be limited or carry penalties. Usually, limited withdrawals are available after year 1 or 2, but the policy is designed to function best when left untouched to grow for at least 5–7 years.

By year 6, most carriers allow you to take policy loans against your cash value on a tax-free basis. These loans don't count as income, which means they don't trigger additional taxes, nor do they increase the taxation of your Social Security benefits. That makes them a powerful tool for supplementing retirement income in a tax-efficient way.

If you *do* need money earlier, you can usually withdraw contributions (your principal) without tax consequences since that's money you already put in after tax. Growth, however, is best left untouched until the loan provisions become available.

Now, if you become sick or disabled, that's a completely different story. Each carrier has its own requirements. Generally, within 90 days of issue, you could tap into the "living benefits" portion.

Q: What happens if I run out of money in my LIRP before I pass away?

A: This is a critical question because if a LIRP lapses with outstanding loans, the IRS treats the unpaid balance as taxable income all at once. That could lead to a massive tax bill in a single year, something no retiree wants.

The good news is that modern LIRPs come with safeguards to prevent this. Many carriers offer features like an "over-loan protection rider," which keeps the policy in force even if loan balances are high relative to cash value. Additionally, a well-trained advisor will structure the policy conservatively, making sure the cash value is always more than sufficient to support loans, insurance costs, and long-term growth.

The bottom line: a properly designed plan should never leave you in the position of running out of money. This is why it's so important to work with an advisor who specializes in tax-free retirement strategies, not just general insurance sales.

Q: How are withdrawals from a LIRP tax-free?

A: The magic of a LIRP lies in how the withdrawals are structured. Unlike a 401(k) or IRA, where distributions are treated as taxable income, LIRP withdrawals are technically structured as *loans*.

Here's how it works:

- You request money from your policy.
- The insurance company lends you the money from its general fund.
- Your cash value serves as collateral for the loan.

- The loan balance is repaid at death from the policy's death benefit.

Since loans are not classified as income, they don't appear on your tax return, and therefore, they don't increase your taxable income or affect Social Security taxation. In essence, you're spending the insurance company's money during retirement, and they're reimbursed later from your policy. This makes the transaction both tax-free and retirement-friendly.

Q: When do I qualify for the 0% loan option?

A: The "0% loan" is a marketing term that refers to a wash loan structure. In reality, the insurance company charges interest on policy loans to keep the transaction "arm's length" for IRS purposes. However, in many contracts, the company credits the *same* amount of interest back to your cash value, creating a net cost of zero.

Most carriers allow this feature beginning in the 6th policy year. This is one reason why patience is important with LIRPs—they're designed for long-term, tax-free retirement income, not as short-term liquidity tools.

Q: What if I need money before the 0% loan option is available?

A: If you need access earlier, you can make partial withdrawals of the money you've put into the policy (your basis). Those contributions can be taken out tax-free, since you already paid taxes on them before funding the LIRP. However, withdrawing earnings early can trigger taxes or penalties, so it's generally recommended to let the plan grow until the loan features become available.

This is why most advisors recommend keeping enough liquidity in taxable or Roth accounts for near-term needs, while letting your LIRP grow undisturbed until it becomes a powerful retirement income engine.

Q: What are the different death benefit options in a LIRP?

A: There are typically two main structures:

- **Option 1 (Level Death Benefit):** The death benefit remains fixed, and as your cash value grows, the insurance portion decreases. This usually lowers the cost of insurance over time, allowing more of your money to compound. Best if looking for ultimate cash accumulation.
- **Option 2 (Increasing Death Benefit):** The death benefit grows as your cash value grows, so the total benefit to your heirs includes both the insurance and the accumulated cash value. This option provides a larger legacy but may come with slightly higher insurance costs.

Choosing the right option depends on your priorities—minimizing costs and maximizing cash value growth (Option 1) versus maximizing the legacy you leave behind (Option 2).

Q: How much can I contribute to a LIRP?

A: Contribution limits in a LIRP aren't capped like they are in Roth IRAs or 401(k)s. Instead, they're linked to the size of your policy's death benefit. The IRS requires that contributions stay within a certain ratio to the death benefit (this is called the "7-pay test"). If you contribute too much too quickly, the policy becomes a Modified Endowment Contract (MEC), losing its tax-free loan treatment.

As a general rule, you can fund up to roughly 20 times your annual income in a death benefit. For high earners, that can translate into very large contributions—hundreds of thousands annually if structured correctly. The flexibility makes LIRPs attractive to people who have maxed out other tax-free retirement accounts.

Q: What happens if I hit a rough patch and can't make contributions for a while?

A: LIRPs are surprisingly flexible. If your policy has built up enough cash value, you can pause or reduce contributions without losing the plan. You can also lower the death benefit temporarily, which reduces the required funding.

Unlike 401(k)s or IRAs, which require contributions to maximize benefits, LIRPs put you in the driver's seat. As long as the policy has enough value to cover insurance charges, it remains in force. That flexibility makes it easier to weather income fluctuations without jeopardizing your retirement plan.

Q: Can I drop a large lump sum—like a bonus or inheritance—into my LIRP?

A: Yes, but you need to be careful. The IRS may require that funding be spread out over several years to prevent overfunding. If you put too much in too quickly, the policy could lose its tax-free treatment.

This is where design matters. A skilled advisor can set up your LIRP to absorb large deposits by adjusting the death benefit and ensuring you don't fail the ***7-pay test*** (MEC) Modified Endowment Contract. After the first seven years, these restrictions loosen, and you typically gain more freedom to add large amounts.

Q: Could the IRS ever change the rules on LIRPs?

A: It's always possible, but historically, when tax laws change, existing contracts are protected by a "grandfather clause." That means if you establish a LIRP under today's rules, you'll continue to enjoy those benefits even if future policies face different restrictions. This is another reason why acting sooner is often smarter: the sooner you lock in today's rules, the more protected you are.

Q: How does the long-term care rider inside a LIRP work?

A: Many modern LIRPs include a rider that allows you to use part of your death benefit to pay for long-term care expenses if you're unable to perform two out of six basic Activities of Daily Living (ADLs), such as bathing, dressing, or feeding yourself.

Instead of paying separately for a stand-alone long-term care policy, you essentially prepay through your LIRP, and any portion you don't use remains as a death benefit for your heirs. This flexibility gives you a safety net for healthcare costs while ensuring your money is still working for you, even if you never need care.

Q: How do I know the insurance company will be around decades from now to honor my LIRP?

A: While no one can predict the future, insurance companies are the most regulated financial institutions in the world. They're required to hold substantial cash reserves, invest conservatively (mostly in bonds), and reinsure their risk with other companies.

Additionally, independent rating agencies like AM Best, Moody's, and Standard & Poor's provide financial strength ratings that reflect an insurer's ability to meet long-term obligations. Choosing a company with high ratings and a long track record provides strong reassurance. In fact, many retirees feel significantly more confident about the stability of an insurance carrier than about banks or stock-driven institutions. Everyone has Homeowners insurance, Health Insurance, and Automobile Insurance. Why not have the same protection and guarantees for your money? Retirement Income Insurance! You never doubt

State Farm wouldn't pay your claim, would you? These Life Insurance companies are 10-15 times the size of State Farm.

Zero Tax Bracket & General Taxes

Q: Isn't it un-American—or unfair—to legally stay in a zero-tax bracket and avoid paying federal taxes?

A: Many people feel that paying no federal income tax sounds "un-American," but the reality is that the U.S. tax code is designed to allow people to minimize taxes *legally*. Structuring your finances to reduce taxes doesn't mean you're cheating; it means you're being a smart taxpayer. A federal judge once said: "*Anyone may arrange their affairs so that their taxes are as low as possible; there is no patriotic duty to increase one's taxes.*"

The bigger picture: paying taxes at historically low rates now is often wiser than deferring or risking higher rates in the future. If you organize your finances strategically, you can pay the *lowest legal tax possible* while still complying fully with the law. Think of it like timing a sale, you wouldn't pay full price if a discount is available. Using today's tax rules to your advantage ensures you're not overpaying, and you remain in full compliance.

A key consideration is flexibility. By keeping most of your qualified money, repositioned in tax-free buckets (Roth IRAs, LIRPs, etc.), you can reduce taxable income in retirement and protect Social Security benefits from taxation. The combination of low taxes now and smart tax-free growth later is a powerful strategy that aligns with both legality and financial prudence.

Q: If it's so advantageous, why doesn't everyone do this?

A: There are several reasons, mostly tied to tradition, financial incentives, and lack of education. Lack of education of the general public and of the advisors. Many financial advisors follow a conventional tax-deferred approach, recommending 401(k)s and traditional IRAs. Why? Because their income depends on managing your assets. Most advisors charge 1%–2% of your portfolio annually, plus commissions on trades. On a $1,000,000 portfolio, that's $10,000–$20,000 per year.

If clients shift funds to tax-free strategies like Roth IRAs or LIRPs, advisors' fees decrease, so many stick with traditional strategies—even if they're not optimal for clients, and it's not.

Another factor is mindset. Most people are taught that saving for retirement means *deferring taxes*, not thinking strategically about withdrawals, tax-free income, or minimizing future liabilities. The truth is that growing your money in a tax-efficient environment is often more important than just growing the balance itself. Different "buckets" of money serve different purposes, and structuring them correctly can save tens or even hundreds of thousands in taxes over a lifetime.

Taxable Bucket – "Today Money"

Q: What happens if I inherit money—does that affect my tax-free strategy?

A: Inheritances usually arrive as cash or liquid assets, which often get deposited into a taxable account by default. This can push you into a higher taxable bracket or disrupt a zero-tax strategy.

The impact depends on factors like:

- Your relationship to the deceased (spouse vs. child vs. non-relative)
- The type of account inherited (taxable, tax-deferred, or Roth)
- Timing of receipt and size relative to your existing taxable income

With careful planning, you can shift inherited assets into tax-free buckets over time, preserving your zero-tax bracket strategy. For example, a surviving spouse can often roll inherited assets into a Roth or LIRP without immediate tax consequences, while children or other heirs may need to plan carefully to avoid unnecessary taxation. Anticipating inheritance timing and amount allows for smoother integration into your retirement strategy.

Q: Is it okay to keep more than 12 months of living expenses in my taxable account?

A: Yes—but it comes at a cost. While having extra liquidity feels safe, keeping too much in a taxable account increases your exposure to taxes and could affect your Social Security benefits. For example, if your taxable account grows large enough, a portion of your Social Security benefits may become taxable.

The key is balance. Maintain enough liquidity for emergencies or short-term goals, but redirect excess funds to tax-free vehicles where possible. This approach maximizes long-term growth and ensures you're not leaving money on the table to unnecessary taxation.

Tax-Deferred Bucket – Someday Money

Q: Should I always contribute to my 401(k) up to my employer's match?

A: Usually, yes—but there are exceptions. Employer matches are essentially "free money," but contributing to a 401(k) can increase your taxable income in retirement if it pushes Social Security or other benefits into higher taxation thresholds.

Sometimes, redirecting money into a tax-free bucket (like a Roth IRA or LIRP) may yield better long-term results. For instance, by paying taxes now on Roth contributions, you may avoid higher taxes later, maintain zero taxation on Social Security, and create a source of flexible, tax-free retirement income.

If you do take an employer match, it's important to have a plan to eventually convert those funds into tax-free growth, either after vesting or during retirement. The balance between tax-deferred contributions and tax-free growth is critical for a tax-efficient retirement strategy.

Roth IRA

Q: Could the government tax my Roth IRA in the future?

A: While nothing is guaranteed, Roth IRAs have historically been protected. Since 1997, the IRS has allowed you to pay taxes on the *seed* now (Roth) rather than the *harvest* later (Traditional IRA). Taxing both would be unprecedented and politically unpopular.

A more realistic concern is future restrictions on contributions for high-income earners. Historically, however, any existing Roth accounts have been grandfathered. Planning around current rules allows you to maximize contributions and take advantage of tax-free growth while minimizing risk.

Q: What is the 5-year rule for Roth IRAs?

A: There are two parts:

- **Contributions:** Withdrawn anytime without penalty or tax.
- **Earnings:** To withdraw growth tax-free, the account must be at least 5 years old, and you must be 59½ or older.

This rule ensures Roth IRAs are used for long-term retirement planning rather than short-term tax benefits.

Q: Can I contribute to a Roth IRA if I work part-time in retirement?

A: Yes, as long as you have earned income. For 2025, contributions for those over 50 can reach $8,000, or $16,000 combined if only one spouse works. Roth IRAs offer flexibility for retirees who continue working part-time, allowing them to build tax-free income even later in life.

ROTH CONVERSIONS

Q: How does the 5-year rule apply to Roth conversions?

A: Each conversion has its own 5-year clock. If under 59½, you must wait 5 years—or until 59½, whichever comes first—to withdraw principal penalty-free. If over 59½, the principal is immediately available, but growth is still subject to the 5-year rule.

This prevents people from using conversions for short-term tax avoidance and encourages long-term planning.

Q: Are there income limits for Roth conversions?

A: No. Anyone can convert, regardless of income. Taxes are owed on the converted amount in the year of conversion. This makes Roth conversions a powerful tool, especially for high earners who want to move money into tax-free buckets. Many financial planners refer to current rates as "taxes on sale"—a chance to lock in low rates while they're still available. As we have covered in the previous chapters of the book, taxes will go up in the future.

Q: Should I convert all at once or spread it out?

A: It depends on your income and tax bracket. A small IRA may be converted entirely without pushing you into a higher bracket. Larger balances often benefit from phased conversions to avoid excessive taxation in a single year. The strategy balances paying taxes now versus risking higher rates in the future.

Ten years from now, you will be more disappointed by the things you did not do... than by the things you did do.

Ten years from now, you'll be 10 years older. Either 10 years older in a ZERO tax retirement or living in the government's tax plan. Your choice.

I truly hope you've enjoyed this book. It's been a pleasure writing it and going down memory lane in a few instances.

This is an exciting time in your life. One that I hope you've been planning on for years, and now have the tax-free mindset and tools to make it stress-free and rewarding.

Go fishing like Bob, take those trips you've always promised to. Learn "something new". Spend more time with family. Get out there and enjoy this period of your life!

Because you're going to implement these ideas in your life, "spend a buck or two" on something or someone special.

Hopefully, you've highlighted several areas in the book and plan to reread it several times. Please share this book with others or buy additional copies as gifts for family and friends you know, or for some who are about to retire. Encourage your children and children of all ages to read this and get on the tax-free train and have **<u>ZERO</u> be everyone's hero!**

Thank you again for your purchase. Blessings to you and yours, and your retirement.

As promised, my email is

taxfreezero@gmail.com

ABOUT THE AUTHOR

Lance A. Mays has over 30 plus years of experience in estate planning, tax-free and tax-advantaged income planning, and all areas of financial services. He has worked for several of the nation's largest insurance and financial services companies at the highest levels. Mays is a Certified Senior Advisor (CSA) member of The Million Dollar Round Table (MDRT), TOP of the Table, and the National Ethics Bureau.

Mays has focused solely on sound, time-proven, conservative retirement strategies that never put clients' hard-earned retirement dollars at risk of loss. Mays has periodically written for different magazines and newspapers. For over 10 years, he hosted a daily National call-in financial talk radio program based out of San Francisco, CA, and then wrapping up in Salt Lake City, Utah, called "Wall Street Meets Main Street".

Tax-Free and Tax-Advantaged Retirement Income Planning, Estate Planning, Estate Asset Protection, Life Insurance, Annuities, Long-Term Care, Life Settlements, and Life Insurance Premium Financing are services provided through licensed and bonded affiliates of West Coast Brokerage (WCI) and AMC Financial Services.

Premium Financing is a specialty service that enables qualified individuals to secure large amounts of life insurance without liquidating their current assets. This product is sought after to obtain larger life insurance policies for the benefit of their families, protecting their estates, and potential estate taxes.

Full Securities Brokerage services are also available through affiliated/referral companies.

Lance A. Mays can be reached at:

taxfreezero@gmail.com

www.ingramcontent.com/pod-product-compliance
Lightning Source LLC
LaVergne TN
LVHW050918210926
848482LV00012B/481
* 9 7 9 8 2 1 8 8 4 7 7 7 7 *